# BROTHER
# MIGUEL
## FEBRES CORDERO, F.S.C.
### TEACHER, SCHOLAR, SAINT

BY LUKE SALM, F.S.C.

Christian Brothers Publications
Romeoville, Illinois

Illustrations

Illustrations by Michael Dundin, F.S.C.
Cover design by Roderick Robertson, F.S.C.

Library of Congress Card Catalog Number: 84-52164

Published by Christian Brothers Publications
100 De La Salle Drive, Romeoville, Illinois 60441 - 1896

Printed by Saint Mary's Press, Winona, Minnesota

# Contents

BROTHER LUKE SALM, a Doctor of Theology, is Professor of Religious Studies at Manhattan College in New York City and Past-President of the Catholic Theological Society of America. An elected delegate to the 39th and 40th General Chapters of the De La Salle Brothers, Brother Luke is currently engaged in making available to a wider public recent scholarly research on the life of St. John Baptist de La Salle and the early history of the Brothers' Institute. Already published are his *Beginnings: De La Salle and His Brothers* (1980) and *Encounters: De La Salle at Parmenie* (1983).

# Foreword

The purpose of these pages is to have readily available in English a short life of Brother Miguel, FSC, on the occasion of his canonization in Rome by Pope John Paul II on October 21, 1984. There is no pretense here to profound scholarship or great originality. This work is based for the most part on the third Spanish edition published in Quito in 1953 of the *Biografía del Siervo de Dios Hermano Miguel de las Escuelas Cristianas* by "a religious of the same congregation." This in turn is a somewhat amplified version of the original biography written in French at Lembec-lez-Hal, Belgium, in 1913, three years after the saint's death. The author has been identified as Brother Paul Joseph, FSC, who came to know Brother Miguel during his stay at Lembecq. As a convenient secondary source, this biography of some 300 closely printed pages contains a considerable amount of historical detail, endless and enthusiastic testimonials from those who knew Brother Miguel and, most valuable of all, generous quotations from the saint's own diaries and letters. Also helpful as a secondary source were two works published in Quito in 1977 when Brother Miguel was beatified along with Brother Mutien-Marie: *Un Académico en los Altares* by Eduardo Muñoz Borrero, FSC, and *Hermano Miguel: Maestro Ejemplar-Amigo y Consejero-Académico Santo* by Luis Páez Fuentes, FSC.

As far as the present writer can ascertain, the only other biography in English is the booklet by Brother Columban M. Cluderay, FSC, entitled *Brother Miguel of Ecuador*. Published in Rome in 1960 on the occasion of the 50th anniversary of Brother Miguel's death, this work of Brother Columban also follows rather closely the French biography of Brother Paul Joseph. It served as a valuable model in English for this present attempt at an updated interpretation. A 16-page summary of Brother Columban's 90-page biography was prepared and published in pamphlet form by Brother Lawrence O'Toole, FSC, former Assistant Superior General for Ireland, on the occasion of the beatification in 1977. Word has filtered through from the motherhouse in Rome that Brother Maurice Auguste, FSC, is preparing a new biography that will be available in time for the canonization and will be published in French, Spanish and English versions. That should not detract from the present study which has been composed primarily with an English-speaking audience in mind and with sensitivity to the style and experience of the Brothers and the Christian community of the church in the United States.

Once the excitement of the canonization has died down and the immediate need for a brief and popular biography, in whatever language, has been met, serious consideration should be given to a new and definitive biography researched to meet the best modern standards of critical scholarship. The source materials are very rich. Not only are all of Brother Miguel's published books available but so also are his diaries, his notebooks and a great number of his personal letters. During his very productive life, he was caught up, however indirectly, in some of the important religious and political movements of the 19th century. His fame as a linguist and philologist was worldwide. All of this suggests that public archives and private collections could yield abundant material to throw new light on the significance of this man for his own time and for ours.

For now, however, we shall have to be content with what has become more or less the standard approach to the story of Brother Miguel. Even so, it is a fascinating tale alternating between the naiveté of a devout soul and the sophistication of an accomplished scholar, the dull routine of a Christian school and the heady excitement of political revolutions. If the reader derives even a small share of the enthusiasm and stimulation that the author found in researching this work, the effort will have proven to be worthwhile.

Thanks are due to Brothers Joseph Schmidt, FSC, and Hilary Gilmartin, FSC, as well as the staffs at the Christian Brothers National Office and Saint Mary's Press for supporting this project and moving it forward; to Brothers Augustine

Loes, FSC, and Gabriel Costello, FSC, for reading the manuscript and for their substantive suggestions for its improvement; to Brother Frederick Altenburg, FSC, of the New York District Archives for valuable assistance in the research; and finally to Brother Edwin Bannon, FSC, of the Generalate Archives in Rome and to Brother John Johnston, FSC, Vicar General, for supplying the most recent data relating to the canonization of Brother Miguel. One hopes that Brother Miguel himself would be pleased at the collaboration of so many of his English-speaking confreres of a latter day. The fact that the work was complete on the solemnity of the Sacred Heart of Jesus, a favorite devotion of his, lends support to that expectation.

Luke Salm, FSC
June 29, 1984
Feast of the Sacred Heart

# BROTHER MIGUEL FEBRES CORDERO, F.S.C.

1854-1910

# I. A New Saint

Amid the awesome splendor and ecclesiastical pomp of the rite of canonization at St. Peter's in Rome, the Holy Father, Pope John Paul II, declares that Brother Miguel, a native of Ecuador and a member of the Institute of the Brothers of the Christian Schools, is now to be honored publicly in the church as a saint. That is the fact, but what does it mean? What, for example, is a saint and what does it mean to canonize one? What is the Institute of the Brothers of the Christian Schools? What kind of place is Ecuador? And, finally, who is this Brother Miguel? The occasion of the canonization in October, 1984, focuses attention on that last question. But it might be well to begin by addressing the others first.

The word *saint*, derived from the Latin *sanctus*, means holy. In the strict sense of the word, God alone is holy, only God is saint. We pray: "Holy, Holy, Holy Lord . . . You alone are the holy One, You alone are the Lord." Yet this holiness of God is not something static within the divinity; it overflows in a dynamic way into all of God's creation. God's Holy Spirit, (*pneuma* in Greek) is inflationary, it is pneumatic. "The Spirit of the Lord fills the whole earth," says the Book of Wisdom. And Jesus, on the night before he died, promised to send this Holy Spirit, the Spirit of truth, upon his disciples. He prayed that his Father would sanctify them in this truth.

For this reason, the New Testament does not hesitate to call all the baptized "saints." That is the way St. Paul addresses the Christians as he writes his letters to the various churches. In Paul's way of expressing it, all Christians are called to be saints by putting on Christ in baptism, by living in Christ and being possessed by his Holy Spirit. Thus, in the first instance, sanctity does not consist in doing something but in being someone: a person accepting in faith God's free gift of grace, a person-to-person communication of the divine life whereby a human being participates in the very holiness of God. Known here on earth only by faith, this dynamic communication of the personal Infinite to finite humans achieves its ultimate realization and fulfillment in the life to come. To be a saint, then, is to be caught up in this process.

From the earliest centuries, some Christians seemed to radiate this participated holiness more obviously than others, either by giving their lives in martyrdom or by the "white martyrdom," as it came to be called, of a lifelong and exemplary fidelity to the person and the cause of Christ. In the beginning of the church's life, it was the spontaneous recognition of the church community that caused the name of this or that heroic Christian to be inscribed in the list of saints, proposed to the rest of the faithful as models of the Christian life and as powerful intercessors before the throne of God for the needs of the church and the world.

As Christianity spread far and wide, with church life and church structure becoming ever more complex, abuses in this matter inevitably began to creep in. The various attempts to reform the process whereby "saints" would be officially recognized as such by the faith community were gradually incorporated into the growing body of the church law, or canon law, as it is known. Hence the term, "canonization." The present legislation governing the process, first of beatification (being declared "blessed") and then canonization (being declared "saint"), dates for the most part from the reforms of Pope Benedict XIV in the 18th century.

The two principal criteria now used in this process are holiness of life and evidence of miracles. Although the procedures for establishing the facts are highly juridical in character, there is a profound theological reason for them. Since God alone is holy, the church wants the best possible human assurance in the face of such a holy mystery that the very life of God has indeed been communicated to this person, this saint if you will, in an extraordinary degree. That is why the virtues practiced by the saint must be shown to be heroic; again, not because sanctity consists in what one does, but rather that the heroic practice of virtue, impossible without the empowerment of divine grace, shows what a person is in terms of the communicated divine life. So it is with the miracles. Problematic as the whole question of physical miracles may be, the search once again is for some clue, some sign from the beyond, some otherwise inexplicable empirical phenomenon, that gives reason to believe that this person's transformation in divine grace continues as an effective reality in eternity. Satisfied on these two scores, the church community can say with conviction, as it did of old, that here is a person who has been an authentic model of the Christian life of grace here on earth and continues as a powerful intercessor before God in heaven.

It is interesting to note that in the examination of "causes" for canonization as they are called, the recent trend seems to put much less emphasis on the documentation of physical miracles, such as medically inexplainable cures, and more on the spontaneous and universal conviction that a saint has indeed been among us. That is itself something awesome and wonderful, which is what the word "miraculous" originally meant. It takes saints to know a saint. If, then, the people of God are a holy people, as the epistle of Peter states, then the holy people of God or a significant segment thereof are the best qualified to recognize and affirm the holiness of one of the members. The collectivity of the "saints" in the church of Ecuador, as St. Paul might have addressed them, and especially the "saints" that comprise the Lasallian family, recognized in Brother Miguel the model of a truly Christian life. And ever since his untimely death they have experienced the power of his heavenly intercession. With this assurance, the Holy Father in the name of the whole church declares the fact with great solemnity and invites the acquiescence of the church universal.

Brother Miguel was a member of the Institute of the Brothers of the Christian Schools, commonly called the Christian Brothers in the United States and the De La Salle Brothers in the rest of the English-speaking world. The Institute was founded in 1680 in the city of Reims in France by St. John Baptist de La Salle. All of the members of the congregation are Brothers devoted exclusively to the work of Christian education. As Brothers, these men are not priests and do not engage in the ministries proper to the ordained clergy. The Brothers do take vows, however, and try in every way to keep alive the spirit of brotherhood among themselves and in relationships with their students.

At the time of their foundation, the Brothers devoted themselves in a special way to the task of providing a sound elementary education for the children of the artisans and the poor who otherwise would have been left without any formal education at all. De La Salle and the early Brothers pioneered in many educational practices that are taken for granted today: simultaneous instruction, lessons given in the vernacular rather than in Latin, special attention to the basic skills of reading and writing, insistence on regular attendance, classroom discipline and sound habits of mental and physical hygiene. By the time of the French Revolution, the Christian Schools of the Brothers had already effected a revolution of sorts in the field of popular education all over France.

A new era in the history of the Brothers began with the restoration of the Institute in France after the French Revolution. During the 36-year term of Brother Philip as Superior General, the followers of De La Salle brought their educational mission to all parts of the world. The Brothers first came to Canada in 1837, the first permanent foundation in the United States was opened in Baltimore in 1845, the first school in London came ten years later in 1855. Then in 1863 the Brothers arrived in Quito in Ecuador, the first foundation in South America. The next on that continent was not to come until 14 years later in Chile; the Brothers did not get to Spain itself until 1878. During this period the number of Brothers grew from about 2,300 in 1838 to more than 10,000 in 1874.

Although some other countries have claimed to be the land of saints and scholars, it is Ecuador that claims our attention as the country of origin of a scholar and now a saint who was known as Brother Miguel. Ecuador, named for the Equator which passes through it, is the smallest but one of the countries of South America. With an area of approximately 115,000 square miles it is slightly larger than the state of Arizona and only slightly smaller than all of Italy. To the north is Colombia; to the east and south, Peru. The western coastal plain facing the Pacific Ocean is intersected by numerous rivers pouring down from the two mountain ranges of the Andes which roughly parallel the coast. These twin ranges – the western and eastern Cordilleras as they are called – comprise hundreds of miles of mountains with more than a dozen peaks over 16,000 feet. Between the Cordilleras there is a vast plateau which itself is more than 7,000 feet above sea level and it is here that the cities and towns associated with Brother Miguel are located. Quito, *La Sultana de los Andes* and the capital city, is just to the north of this plateau. Finally, on the eastern side there is the Oriente, a tropical region of dense forest and jungle that occupies almost half the area of the country.

Impressive as it is in its geography, Ecuador's population by comparison is rather small, about 8,300,000 people according to the most recent census figures. Of these about 30 percent are Indians, about 15 percent are white, mostly of Spanish descent, and the rest are Mestizos of mixed Caucasian and Indian blood.

The Spanish conquest of Ecuador began in earnest in the early 16th century under the leadership of Sebastián de Benalcázar. After the fierce fighting on the coastal plain, he pushed on to Quito only to find it razed to the ground by the retreating Indians. Here in 1534 he founded the new city of San Francisco de Quito, naming it in honor of his own brother and fellow explorer, Francisco. For the next 300 years Ecuador would be part of the Spanish Empire. Following the military invasion came the priests and nuns to preach the gospel, the traders and colonists to seek their fortunes, and so to give to the spiritual, intellectual, social and political life of the country its dominantly Hispanic character.

The movement towards national independence began in the early years of the 19th century. Allied with Colombia and Venezuela under the leadership of Simón Bolívar, Ecuador achieved its independence from Spain in 1822, content at first to be part of the Confederation of Gran Colombia with her two allies. In 1830 Ecuador became an independent republic. The early days of the newly independent state were stormy ones, the first president being assassinated even before he could take office. It was only after 30 years, under the enlightened leadership of García Moreno from 1860 to 1875, that a more settled state of affairs began to prevail, not the least part of which was a stabilization of the relations between church and state through a concordat with the Vatican.

It was this García Moreno who first arranged to have the Christian Brothers come to Ecuador to open schools there. He was statesman enough to realize that the future stability and prosperity of his country would depend on a sound system of education which at that time was totally lacking in Ecuador. Fortunately, his chief adviser in church affairs was Don José Ordóñez, Archdeacon of Cuenca and later Archbishop of Quito. Having studied for the priesthood in Paris at the Seminary of Saint Sulpice, he had seen the work of the Brothers there at firsthand. At the request of President Moreno, he opened negotiations with the Superior General of the Institute, the famous Brother Philip, for a number of Brothers to be sent to Ecuador. After some months of preparation learning Spanish, on February 1, 1863, a group of ten Brothers set sail from Southampton on the ship *La Plata* bound for South America. A few weeks later they disembarked at Colón, crossed the isthmus to Panama City and finally arrived at Guayaquil, the main port of Ecuador on February 28. The next day was the first of the month dedicated to St. Joseph and so it seemed appropriate for the Brothers, after Mass and Communion, to place their mission under the protection of that special patron of the Institute.

According to plan, the Brothers then divided into three groups. Four of them with Brother Albanus, who had been appointed by the Superior General to be Director and Provincial, went to Quito; three others went to Cuenca, and the remaining three remained in Guayaquil. It was the last of these groups that had the most difficulty. The climate of the port city was not very healthy, surrounded as it was with malarial marshes, and the people of the locality proved hostile to the newcomers. After a short time these Brothers left to join those at Cuenca; a community was not finally established in Guayaquil until some years later.

The Brothers in Quito settled down at once. A former convent school known as the Beaterio was put at their disposal. Although it lacked many conveniences, it was at least a place to live and work in and it was ready-made for school purposes. Incredible as it may seem, the records indicate that within a few days the school had already enrolled more than 200 pupils. There is also evidence that the small community had to endure many a trial. They did not escape the suspicion and distrust which are the usual reaction to newcomers. Unused to the climate, ignorant of the local customs and temperament, and not very proficient in the language, the Brothers had to learn by experience the best methods to educate children whose background was so completely unknown to them.

The Brothers at Cuenca seem to have fared the best of all. From the outset everything had gone well with the new school provided for them, and it seems that for the most part they were spared the trials and tribulations that plagued their Brothers in Guayaquil and Quito. The city of Cuenca is beautifully situated at an altitude of some 7,000 feet and is surrounded by some of the most spectacular scenery and fertile countryside in the whole world. The climate is pleasant and healthy. Superlatives are used to describe Cuenca – the city of perpetual Spring, the Athens of the Equator, and, because of its special religious devotion, the city of the Blessed Sacrament. When in 1863 the six French Brothers opened their school in Cuenca, they had no way of knowing that among their first pupils was one who would bring new fame to the city as the birthplace of the saint from Ecuador, Brother Miguel.

# II. Childhood

The future Brother Miguel was born Francisco Febres Cordero Muñoz in Cuenca, Ecuador, on November 7, 1854. Just one month later the town of Cuenca celebrated with great enthusiasm the proclamation of the dogma of the Immaculate Conception of Mary by Pope Pius IX on December 8 of that year. Later on, Brother Miguel would often remark that he considered this coincidence as a special sign that his life would be under Mary's protection.

The family of the young Francisco was distinguished in many ways. His grandfather was a famous general, León Febres Cordero, one of the heroes in the struggle for Ecuador's independence. The father, Francisco Febres Cordero Montoya, came originally from Guayaquil. A man of great charm and culture, fluent in five languages, he was prominent in the troubled political affairs of the country. At the time of Francisco's birth he was a professor of English and French at the seminary college at Cuenca. The mother was Ana Muñoz, one of 19 children of an influential Cuencan family, five of whom became nuns and one a Jesuit priest. Throughout her life she was known as a woman of intelligence and industry, combining a gentle disposition with a deep religious faith. Not only did she provide for the religious education of her own children, but as time went on she became increasingly involved in charitable works in favor of the poor and those suffering from incurable disease. This influence of a learned father and a devout mother provided the kind of home environment from which would emerge the scholar saint.

But that did not happen all at once or without considerable difficulty. For one thing, Francisco was a delicate child with crippled legs that caused the family to doubt that he would ever be able to walk. Unfortunately, the father took this rather badly and let it be known that he expected this son of his to be a burden and an invalid for the rest of his life. His mother, on the other hand, watched over him with tender care and kept alive the hope that one day little Panchito, as he was affectionately called, would grow up to be healthy and strong. Meanwhile the child learned from the mother to accept his sufferings with a smile and offer them to God.

It was from his mother, too, that the prayer life of the young lad began to assume a definite shape. As was customary in Catholic devotional practice at the time, God and the saints were envisioned and addressed as if they were familiar members of the household. To young Francisco, Jesus, Mary and Joseph seemed as accessible as if they were in the next room or, certainly, no farther away than the next town. In effect, the members of the Holy Family became personal friends of his. All his life he would speak to them and even write to them in that vein, always anxious to do what would please them, to sacrifice for them, to avoid hurting their feelings and to atone for his own lapses and those of the others who seemed not to care. Even from his earliest childhood Francisco reserved a privileged place in his religious imagination for his heavenly Mother Mary as a special object of his veneration and love.

This sense of familiarity with his heavenly patrons lends some credence to an incident that took place when Francisco was not quite five years old. At the time he happened to be at home under the care of his Aunt Asunción. He was looking out at the garden from an upstairs window when suddenly his eyes lit up and he began to stare fixedly at the roses on the patio. His face was radiant. "Auntie, Auntie," he called as if from far away, "come see the beautiful lady there near the roses." Trying to hide her excitement, Asunción said calmly, "Well, then, Panchito, ask her to come in." Scarcely listening he continued, "How beautiful she looks in her white dress and blue mantle! Can't you see her? She is calling to me and wants me to come to her." And then, for the first time in his life, he began to walk. As he stepped forward towards the lady, she smiled once more and then disappeared, whereupon he tumbled to the floor. Whatever other explanations may be given for this event, Doña Asunción remained convinced that it was the Queen of Heaven who had appeared to the child. Doña Ana, on the other hand, was fearful that the words, "she wants me to come to her," might forebode the untimely death of her dear son. In any event, another year passed before Francisco walked again, but from this time on his general health began to improve.

*"Auntie, Auntie, come see the beautiful lady there near the roses."*

When circumstances required that both father and mother should leave Cuenca for an extended stay in Guayaquil, they entrusted Francisco to the care of Asunción who treated him as one of her own sons. By the time he was eight years old, Francisco became strong enough to walk and play in games that were not too strenuous. One day he set off with his two cousins for an outing in the fields. Their games were interrupted by the appearance of a wild bull which began to charge at them. The two other boys ran away quickly, but Francisco was unable to do so. Instead he lay down and kept perfectly still, praying the while to his heavenly protectress. The bull looked him over, prodded him a bit and then stalked away. A narrow escape that the boy attributed not so much to his own good sense as to Mary's protection and care.

There are other incidents that the biographers relate in order to highlight, as was customary in an older style of hagiography, any indication of precocious sanctity or special divine favor. Thus Francisco was said to have special love for daily Mass, he was devoted to the Rosary, he liked to listen to the lives of the saints and even tried to act out in his childish way some of their penances, he avoided girls as playmates, he enjoyed making toy altars. Such things are really not so very unusual for a delicate child reared in a protected and strongly religious environment. More significant is one element that is often cited in the biographies. He was a happy and carefree child with a sunny smile and an affectionate nature. In more mature form, these qualities along with his piety would remain characteristic of him all through his life.

Francisco was educated at home until he was nine years old. When, in 1863, the Brothers opened their new school at Cuenca he was one of the first to be enrolled. He liked the Brothers very much and from the very first day he was attracted by their humble way of life and the devotion they brought to their apostolate of religious education. The Brothers in turn quickly realized that they had a pupil of rare intelligence and genuine religious spirit. Francisco was always among the leaders of his class and enjoyed the friendly rivalry with the two or three others who shared his zeal for study and exactness in completing assignments. His fine character and cheerful manner endeared him to everyone. It would even happen, when the pain in his legs made it difficult for him to walk to school, that some of his companions would help to carry him part of the way.

It wasn't long before Francisco was appointed class monitor to keep an eye on things when a Brother had to be absent. The other boys respected him because he always acted on principle and with complete fairness. However, one lad had it in for him and falsely accused him of a breach of discipline for which he was punished. The next time Francisco was on duty as monitor, this same youngster instigated a major disturbance that involved many other boys. Francisco reported them all except the leader. When the Brother finally got to the heart of the matter, he asked Francisco why he had not reported the boy as the chief culprit. "Because," he said, "he had reported me only the other day, and I did not want to try to get even."

Not long afterwards the President of the Republic of Ecuador, Gabriel García Moreno, came to Cuenca and took the occasion to visit the school of the Brothers. Francisco was chosen to represent his fellow students and to greet the President in their name. The speech of welcome was delivered in Spanish and in French. The President, a man known not to be easily pleased, was so impressed that he heaped upon the young orator words of the most fulsome praise. From that time on García Moreno never lost track of this promising young student. Years later he was to show his appreciation by helping to rescue Brother Miguel's father from a compromising political situation.

As time went on it became a particular source of pleasure for Francisco to remain after school with the Brothers. He would spend the time studying his lessons, completing his written exercises and, as opportunity presented itself, offering to help the Brothers in any way that he could. He would stay until late in the afternoon, going home only when one of his family's servants came to call for him. Although he returned willingly enough to the family, he considered the Brothers' community his second home and a source of contentment that nothing could rival or take away. Though still in his early teens, the road to the future was beginning to open up for this unusual young man.

20

# III. Vocation

Like many a young man before and since, it was the initial and close contact with the Brothers that convinced Francisco, almost from the start, that God was indeed calling him to share the life and the apostolate of the sons of De La Salle. In the mature reflection of his later years, Brother Miguel expressed it in his own words:

*From the moment I entered the school of the Brothers, God gave me a burning desire one day to be clothed in the holy habit of the Institute. I always enjoyed being among the Brothers. I used to make spiritual reading with them and sometimes I was allowed to join with them in the Office of the Blessed Virgin and the Office of the Dead, though some of the members of my family were not happy that I did so.*

*My teachers were Brothers Junianus and Adelphus. But more than any other it was the Brother Director who made an impression on me, so devoted was he to our instruction and education. Despite his bad health and infirmities, he never abandoned us, though often, when he was crippled with rheumatism, he had to be carried into class in a chair in order to be with us.*

*He frequently talked to us of Our Lord, of our good Mother Mary, and of Saint Joseph, and gave us a great love for them. During catechism he taught us to love virtue and to hate sin, stressing the need to avoid bad companions. His success as a teacher was due not to severity but to trusting us on our honor and by showing kindness. One look from him was enough to bring a recalcitrant to tears and reformation. I firmly believe that God made use of him and his example to give me a great love for the religious life.*

The desire of Francisco to join the Brothers was not to be met easily or all at once. When he announced his intentions at home the news was greeted with a rather cold reception. Even his pious mother was not too enthusiastic. His father, resident for the time being in Lima for business reasons, was even more opposed. The most fearsome opposition came from the grandmother, Doña Mercedes Cárdenas, who envisioned for Francisco a distinguished career as a preacher in one of the great religious orders or, perhaps, as a learned theologian with a top position in the seminary. She thought of the Brothers as poor and unknown, foreigners to boot, with a very uncertain future in the country. His parents were convinced that he was too delicate to consider such a life and so, for the time being at least, he was asked to forget about the Brothers.

In the hope of changing his outlook, the family arranged to have him enter as a boarder in the seminary of Cuenca. To Francisco this was a cruel blow and every day was a torment. Years later, he was to describe this experience:

*I remained at the seminary for only three months but it seemed to me like three centuries. I suffered a great deal in my heart, even though the teachers and the other students showed me every consideration. It simply was not the place where God wanted me to be and I was like a fish out of water.*

*One of my uncles who was very fond of me used to visit me and give me money to buy treats for myself. Actually he was trying to bribe me into staying in the seminary. But by an inspiration of my heavenly Mother, the Immaculate Virgin Mary, I used this money to buy candles to burn before her statue. I entreated her constantly in this way to rescue me from this purgatory and to help me on the road to following my true vocation.*

Soon the nervous strain and sense of frustration began to take their toll. Frequent and violent headaches lead to a general deterioration in Francisco's health. In his repeated visits to the rector of the seminary, he was firm in his request: "Please help my mother understand," he would say, "that I am not where God wants me to be. I am dying of unhappiness." At length his mother gave in, and he was allowed to go back to the Brothers' school.

Once he was back among the Brothers, Francisco urged the Brother Director to arrange to have him enter the Institute. The Director wrote to the father in Lima and received this reply:

*It was with much pleasure that I received your letter in which you request that I give permission for my son to follow the vocation of a Brother of the Christian Schools . . . .*

*Be assured that I shall never stand in the way of my son following whatever career he believes is his true calling. That would be criminal on my part. I want to give him full freedom of choice in this matter. However, since he is still so young, I think there should be some delay before he comes to a final decision.*

The letter is dated September 13, 1867, when Francisco was just approaching his 14th year. The delay lasted for the next several months until even the grandmother finally began to change her mind. In the long run, it was the mother who gave her formal consent, realizing that her son's happiness was at stake.

And so it was that Francisco finally entered the Brothers' house at Cuenca to prepare by prayer and study for the taking of the religious habit. That happy event took place on March 24, 1868, the eve of the feast of the Annunciation, when the young Francisco was clothed in the black robe and white rabat of the De La Salle Brothers and given the name Brother Miguel. He was only 14 at the time, a very young age indeed, but this was the period before the Code of Canon Law of 1917 set the minimum age at 16.

The following months were spent in making the novitiate, a period when every young Brother receives his basic training in the religious life. A full year is devoted to the practice of mental prayer and the other religious exercises, the study of the Rules and Constitutions of the Institute, the life and spirit of the Founder, Saint John Baptist de La Salle, and the meaning and obligations of the vows that the Brother would soon be asked to pronounce. At the time there was no special house of novitiate in Ecuador. The Brothers had opened one briefly in Quito, but after the few Ecuadorians who had presented themselves departed one by one it had to be closed. At first the Brothers thought of sending Brother Miguel to France to make his novitiate at the center of the Institute, but his delicate constitution made this impractical. Accordingly permission was obtained for this first Ecuadorian Brother to make his novitiate in the community of the Brothers at Cuenca.

The prayerful and serene atmosphere of the novitiate year was rudely disturbed when his father wrote from Guayaquil asking that Brother Miguel come there to spend a few days with the rest of the family. The superiors were in no position to grant such a request so totally contrary to the discipline common to all religious institutes for the year of the novitiate. Although the Brothers tried to make the reasons for the refusal clear and to phrase them in the most tactful language, the father refused to be convinced or satisfied. As a result there began a long and painful break in the relationship between father and son that was to prove a considerable burden for the next several years.

Otherwise, the year of novitiate passed quickly. Early in May, 1869, Brother Miguel received his first assignment. He left Cuenca on horseback in the company of a mule driver who served as his guide and arrived at Quito a few days later. There he was put in charge of the third class in the Beaterio. But trouble lay ahead. He was in Quito only three days when the Brother Provincial received a very strong letter from his father demanding this time that his son should leave the Institute altogether. He indicated that a Señor Caamaño, a member of the government, would call for his son and bring him back at once to Guayaquil.

The reply of the Brother Provincial was gracious but firm. In a letter dated May 22, 1869, he wrote as follows:

*My dear Sir: In reply to your very courteous letter of the fifteenth of this month, I have the honor to inform you that for my part I am disposed to hand over your son Francisco to whatever person you may designate, but always on condition that the young man himself feels that it is in his best interest to leave the Institute into which he was received a year ago on the basis of the reasons he gave for seeking admission.*

*I could not possibly, without serious injustice, dismiss him from our house against his will. The young man himself will have to decide what he ought to do according to the dictates of his conscience and the demands of justice.*

*It is not necessary that you try to repay us for the great care we have taken to educate your esteemed son. That is one of our first obligations and one that we are proud to retain in the Institute of the Brothers of the Christian Schools.*

*I am pleased to take this occasion to offer you my humble and sincere greetings in the Lord.*

The Brother Provincial also wrote to Brother Miguel asking him to consider the matter seriously and to reply within three days.

The reply of Brother Miguel left no doubt as to his mind in the matter:

*My dear Brother Provincial: In reply to your very kind letter, I wish to assure you in the presence of God and without any human consideration that I believe that I have been called by God to the Institute of the Brothers of the Christian Schools and that I could not be sure of my salvation or even be content in any other walk of life.*

*I should be very grateful, therefore, my very esteemed Brother Provincial, if you would communicate my feelings in this matter to my father. If he truly desires my happiness, in other words my eternal salvation, something that every Christian parent should want for his children, he will not persist any longer in trying to prevent me from following the road that God has marked out for me with unmistakable signs.*

The Brother Provincial also sought the opinion of the Apostolic Delegate and the Archbishop of Quito, both of whom agreed that Brother Miguel should remain in the Institute if that was his wish.

The result of all this was that Señor Febres Cordero refused to have anything more to do with his son. This sad state of affairs lasted for the next six years when it was resolved in a most unexpected way. In January, 1875, when García Moreno was up again for re-election, an opposition party was formed with its center in Guayaquil. The suppression of the radical periodical, *La Era Nueva*, resulted in the arrest of several leaders of the opposition. Among the prisoners detained in the capital was a Doctor Arízaga, a personal friend of Señor Febres Cordero. Realizing how much his own political views were at variance with those of the President, Señor Febres Cordero felt helpless to aid his imprisoned friend. But he knew of President García Moreno's high regard for the Brothers, so he contacted his son through a third party, and assured Brother Miguel that if he could obtain the release of Doctor Arízaga, all of the past bitterness would be forgotten. Brother Miguel went with the Brother Provincial to see the President who assured them that he would honor their request.

The President himself was quite aware of the resentment that the father felt toward Brother Miguel and apparently he wanted to do what he could to remedy the situation. In any event, on February 20, 1875, Brother Miguel received from his father a touching letter expressing his deep gratitude for the release of Doctor Arízaga and granting his paternal blessing with heartfelt affection.

Over the next several years the father continued to be active in Ecuadorian politics, usually in the opposition party, but his communications with his son remained frequent and cordial. After a short illness and a devout reception of the last sacraments, Señor Febres Cordero died on July 16, 1882.

On December 8 of the same year in which his father died, Brother Miguel put the final seal on his vocation by pronouncing his perpetual vows of chastity, poverty and obedience as well as the two special vows proper to the Brothers, stability and teaching gratuitously. Two extraordinary events marked the occasion. He composed a lengthy poem entitled, "An Ode on the Day of My Profession," one of the few that he published and one that is often found in anthologies of Ecuadorian literature. A few stanzas are quoted here in Spanish and English with the realization that much of the beauty is lost in translation:

| | |
|---|---|
| No te bastó llamarme | It was not enough that you |
| De tus hijos, ¡oh Dios! a la alta | called me, O God, from among |
| herencia | all your sons, to a noble and |
| Preciosa, y libertarme | precious heritage. You have |
| De la fatal demencia | freed me from the fatal mad- |
| En que corre del mundo la | ness that prevails in the world. |
| existencia. | |
| | |
| También con lazo fuerte | Today also you have bound me |
| Hoy a tu triunfal carro me has | by a strong rope and a knot |
| atado | to your triumphal retinue, so |
| Con nudo hasta la muerte, | that without any other care, I |
| Porque esté sin cuidado | shall be sheltered unto death. |
| En asilo seguro resguardado. | |
| | |
| Nobilísimos lazos | The noblest bonds of chastity, |
| De castidad, pobreza y obediencia | poverty and obedience, while |
| Que, atándome los brazos, | they keep my body in check, |
| abrís a mi conciencia | you open to my mind the nar- |
| Camino ancho y seguro, y | row and secure road that leads |
| clara ciencia. | to true wisdom. |

Also, on that same day, Brother Miguel wrote a surprising letter to an aunt of his who was a religious of the Sacred Hearts of Jesus and Mary. He intimated to her that by some special illumination he knew for certain that his father had already entered into heavenly glory. He interpreted this special grace as a reward that had been given to him for being faithful to his vocation.

# IV. Teacher

When Brother Miguel arrived in Quito in 1869 to begin his teaching career in the third class at the Beaterio, he was only 15 years old.

The school itself had been in existence for only six years but it was already beginning to prosper. It seems that from the outset Brother Miguel was a great success as a teacher. He made the usual mistakes of a beginning teacher – it is reported that at first he talked too much, made too many gestures and gave in too readily to laughter. But these defects were quickly turned into strengths as he deliberately set out to make his lessons as interesting as possible. "I must," he wrote in one of his diaries, "look for every possible way of making the lessons and work agreeable and pleasant for the pupils."

He was also a realist. He learned early on not to expect too much of himself or his pupils. He wrote: "Teachers must expect industrious pupils and lazy pupils, those who are attentive and those easily distracted. Sometimes students are careful, sometimes careless. That is the way young children are. We must put up with their moods patiently and not show annoyance. It is useless and even dangerous to be continually nagging children for being scatterbrained and unable to concentrate." It was with this sort of outlook that Brother Miguel entered into a distinguished career in the classroom that was to last for the next 38 years.

One secret of Brother Miguel's success as a teacher was the importance he gave to the careful preparation of his lessons. He himself had always been a good student and a lover of books and so this came easily to him. The story is told that in his later years a young Brother came upon him as he was busily preparing one of his classes. "Brother Miguel," he said, "you have been teaching that same material for 20 years. Why are you working so hard to prepare it?" The reply was characteristic: "That is true. Of course I know it – or I think I know it. But I also think that I can find a better way of presenting it every year. I'm sure that if I teach this material for another 20 years, I will still find even newer and better ways of explaining it." On another occasion he put it this way: "When a chef has created a perfect dish he is happy to serve it at table. It is the same with a teacher who has prepared his lessons with care."

In addition to preparing the subject matter with care, Brother Miguel was just as concerned to adapt his lessons to the mindset of his pupils. He studied their reactions carefully and took written notes of their replies to his questions and the difficulties they had in understanding the material. He liked to mingle with the boys at play after school hours, listening attentively to their schoolboy idiom so as to better conform to their own way of expressing themselves. His lessons, as a result, were models of good organization and clear exposition, presented in simple language and spiced with concrete examples drawn from the pupils' world of experience. It was said of him that his aim was not to be brilliant but to be understood. One Brother expressed his personal conviction that "teaching was a joy to Brother Miguel and his classes were a joy to his pupils."

In his determination "to discover every possible way of making school attractive," Brother Miguel was helped immeasurably by his own personality, his calm disposition and his winning ways. One of his former pupils, who later became a priest, had this to say of him: "It was his great charm of manner that drew us to him and we were always delighted to be with him at any time. One of the great things about him is that he never made any distinction between the rich and poor but treated everyone alike. It always struck me that he genuinely enjoyed being among us and we certainly loved to be with him. I never once saw him being harsh or even impolite to anyone. All the boys in the school loved him." Other former students remembered the fact that "nobody ever saw him impatient or moody for he was always calm and even tempered. Brother Miguel maintained in all circumstances an amazing serenity and calm."

It must not be thought, however, that this exterior serenity and calm came easily or without effort. It is enough to reflect on the demands of the daily grind. In those days the Brothers rose at 4:30 AM, devoted a full hour to vocal and mental prayer, and then attended daily Mass. This was followed by long hours

*"Teaching was a joy to Brother Miguel and his classes were a joy to his pupils."*

in the school (with no "free periods"), mingling with the boys after school, and then returning to the community for more prayer and spiritual reading. After supper and a brief period of recreation, it was time to prepare for the next day's classes. Furthermore, Brother Miguel himself did not enjoy good health. He suffered constantly from severe headaches and had permission from the superiors to use snuff to bring some measure of relief. His crippled legs and a generally weak constitution left him prey to many minor ailments. Yet it was said of him that he never wasted a minute; he was always working and looking for work.

In these circumstances, how remarkable it is that in 1873, when he was not yet 20 years old and had been teaching for only four years, Brother Miguel managed to publish the first of his many books, a Spanish grammar, a book of such quality that within a year it was the prescribed text for all the schools of Ecuador. During the next few years he published seven other educational works: an elementary reader, a book of Spanish lessons, a Life of Christ, a text in literature, an abridged Spanish grammar, a translation of De La Salle's work on Christian politeness, and an anthology of readings.

It is no wonder that by the time he was 30 he had aged considerably and looked frail and worn out. Yet despite all this, he was known as the smiling Brother with the twinkling eyes, at all times seeming to be perfectly relaxed and bubbling over with good humor. Although the secret of his sanctity lay well concealed, we know from his diaries that his happiness was not feigned. It came from deep within himself, profoundly content to be doing always what he was convinced God wanted him to do.

It was in the religion class above all that Brother Miguel found the greatest source of his joy and the most intense awareness of his apostolic vocation to do the work of the Lord. In the early days of the 20th century, Pope Pius X designated the De La Salle Brothers as the Apostles of the Catechism, and indeed they were. From the time of their Founder it was taken for granted that every Brother who taught at all would teach religion and be involved with the religious formation of his students.

In addition to the formal religion class there was a prescribed prayer schedule for the students that included the recitation of the Rosary and the recollection of the presence of God on the hour and the half hour. Each Brother was required to give a daily "reflection," a personal and pointed exhortation to the students to rise to the demands of the gospel. The presentation of Christian doctrine was straightforward and uncomplicated; what had to be believed was clearly spelled out, as were also those actions that were considered sin and what means had to be taken to avoid the occasions. Although importance was attached to the reception of the sacraments and attendance at liturgical services, greater attention by far was paid to popular devotions: to the Sacred Heart, to Jesus in the Blessed Sacrament, to Mary under her various titles, to the "great" St. Joseph and to the patron saints. The driving motive behind all of this catechetical activity and religious formation was the conviction, supported by the theology of the time, that the eternal salvation of the students depended on their acceptance of church doctrine and discipline.

From the distance of 100 years and in a totally different religious and cultural milieu, it is not easy to make comprehensible the impact that Brother Miguel had as a catechist and a teacher of religion. His Latin-American biographers devote whole chapters to the special care he gave to preparing his students to receive their first Holy Communion, which in the church's discipline of those days was not available to youngsters until their early teens.

His former students describe the enormous impact this holy man had on their religious outlook and their lives. Quite clearly it was the authenticity of the personal faith of Brother Miguel that had such an influence for good on his students. If his devotional approach to the divine mysteries and his sense of intimacy with his heavenly patrons might be viewed today as theologically naive, there can be no question that it was genuine and was communicated as such to the young lads fortunate enough to have him as a model and guide for their religious formation.

Apart from the religion classes, those which Brother Miguel enjoyed the most and which had the greatest success were his classes in Spanish. He taught Spanish in its purest Castilian form. In this regard, his good friend and mentor, the famous Colombian poet, Belisario Peña, is our best source: "Brother Miguel has no equal as a professor of the Castilian tongue. He understands its roots and he knows how to teach his students, little by little, the richness of this most beautiful Spanish idiom. One of the qualities that I most admire in him is the way in which he corrects in our young Ecuadorians the rudeness of their speech and the consistency by which he exemplifies in his own manner of speaking this language as a model of correct usage, simplicity, subtlety and distinctiveness. Without any doubt, he is a master."

In view of this growing realization among the educated community of Quito that a true educator was to be found in their midst, it is not surprising that official recognition should come in the appointment of Brother Miguel as a public examiner and inspector for the schools of Quito. Although he was wary of public display, this new assignment required that he be present regularly for the trimester oral examinations which were significant events in the life of the city. These occasions were presided over by a representative of the government, and places of honor were given to the professors and directors of the local colleges. Present and much in evidence were the parents of the young scholars. Brother Miguel was by far the favorite among the examiners. He knew how to ask the right questions, how to put the students at ease, how to engage them in argument, so that they could show off to best advantage what they had learned. He was always happiest, it seems, when one of the students got the better of him in the debate. Thus in public, as well as in the classroom, Brother Miguel manifested the awareness possessed by every good teacher: the youngsters being educated are more important than the subject matter they are expected to learn.

During this period, as Brother Miguel was developing into a master teacher, the school itself was prospering. When Brother Miguel arrived in Quito in 1869, there were 250 pupils in the Beaterio; by 1875 the number had increased to 1,000. This was due in no small measure to the initiative and support of President García Moreno. Already in 1869 he had written a let-

"*He genuinely enjoyed being among us and we certainly loved to be with him.*"

ter in his own hand to Brother Philip, the Superior General in Paris, asking for no less than 35 additional Brothers. Although the Superior was unable to supply even half that number, he promised to send as many Brothers as could be spared from the schools and colleges of France. The arrival of these new recruits from France, together with a small number of Ecuadorian novices, enabled the Brothers to expand their work considerably. Schools were opened in 1870 at Latacunga and Guayaquil, and in succeeding years in other cities, including one in Pasto, Colombia, in 1875. Thus, after a dozen years, the Ecuador province of the Institute had seven schools, a novitiate, 50 Brothers and 4,000 pupils.

The year 1875, however, marked a turning point in the affairs of the Brothers in Ecuador. On August 6 of that year the President, Gabriel García Moreno, was assassinated in the public square in Quito. The Brothers thus lost a powerful protector and benefactor, one whom they had made an affiliated member of their Institute. His immediate successor, however, was just as supportive to the Brothers and a personal friend of Señor Cordero, the father of Brother Miguel. Unfortunately this new President was replaced within a year by General Veintimilla at the head of a more revolutionary government. In the political unrest that followed it seemed as if the Brothers might be forced to close their schools. Uncertain of their fate as foreigners, many of them were thinking of leaving the country.

To deal with the crisis, Brother Irlide, who had succeeded Brother Philip as Superior General, sent a Delegate from France with the authority to make any necessary decisions on the spot. Much to the Delegate's surprise, President Veintimilla not only refused to allow any Brothers to leave the country but he even threatened to impose a heavy fine by way of indemnity for any Brother who abandoned his post. "You tell your Superior General," he said, "that we intend to hold to the letter of all the provisions of the contract the government has made with the Brothers." Thus reassured, the Brothers gave up their plans to leave Ecuador. Things returned more or less to normal for the next several years, although now in a more hostile and volatile political climate.

35

# V. Scholar

As the years rolled by it was inevitable that the rare combination in Brother Miguel of a keen intelligence, a charming and effective classroom presence, and an authentic religious spirit would soon make him outstanding among his Brothers and bring him to the attention of the public at large. The occasion presented itself when, in 1887, it was announced that a date had been set in the following year for the beatification of John Baptist de La Salle, the Founder of the Brothers' Institute. This news brought joy to the Brothers all over the world, not least of all to those in Ecuador where they learned that one of their number was to be designated to represent them at Rome. The choice fell upon Brother Miguel and it was unanimously applauded. Despite the fact that he was not one of the superiors, it was evident to all that as a native Ecuadorian and a very talented person, Brother Miguel could best represent that part of the Institute. Not only was he the most distinguished member of the Brothers' community and an exemplary religious, but he had also become identified with the Founder through his translations into Spanish of the life of De La Salle and some of his writings.

Brother Miguel set out on the long journey to Rome in November, 1887, in the company of Doctor Carlos Tobar, the Director of the Ecuadorian Academy. The trip began with a seven-day trek on horseback over the mountains to the port of Guayaquil. Then came the sea voyage to Panama, overland again to Colón, and from there across the Atlantic to Saint Nazaire in France. It was Miguel's first experience at sea. His poetic spirit was thrilled by the beauty of the ocean and the majestic power of the waves, while his religious sensitivity rejoiced at this most awesome manifestation of the beauty and power of the Creator. But his delight was not to last long. He quickly fell victim to seasickness and not even the friendly and medical ministrations of his solicitous companion could alleviate his suffering, as anyone who has been through the same experience can readily understand.

Arrived finally in France, Brother Miguel remained in Paris for a while to arrange some of the details connected with the translation and publication of Institute writings that he was preparing for South America. He arrived in Rome early in February, 1888. On February 19 he had the great joy of being present when Pope Leo XIII solemnly proclaimed that John Baptist de La Salle was to be numbered and honored among the Blessed in heaven. The beatification ceremony took place in the large hall above the main portico of St. Peter's which was generally used at that time for such ceremonies. It was decorated with huge tapestries depicting the life of De La Salle and the miracles worked through his intercession. The relics of De La Salle were given a prominent place in the display.

Present were 14 cardinals; 20 bishops; Brother Joseph, the Superior General, with his Brother Assistants; and more than 200 Brothers from countries all over the world. Brother Miguel later described his experience in these words: "There I was," he said, "an unknown Brother from Ecuador who never would have dreamed of making a pilgrimage to Rome. Being there, I felt as if I had been carried up into the third heaven!" He went on to say that he had prepared many prayers and petitions to address to heaven, but all he could do in that unforgettable moment was to say to his Lord: "Thank you for the Institute, thank you for myself. For the rest, O Lord, you already know all my petitions."

Although Brother Miguel was understandably impressed by the ceremony and the dignitaries present, it is interesting to note in passing how modest it seems in comparison with the scene in St. Peter's Square when Brother Miguel himself, together with Brother Mutien-Marie, was beatified in 1977. On that occasion there were twice as many prelates, 20 concelebrants, 100 priests to distribute Communion, literally hundreds of Brothers (100 in the choir alone), and tens of thousands of pilgrims in attendance.

Brother Miguel remained in Rome for three more weeks with

plenty of opportunity to give free rein to his religious imagination. He was enough of a scholar and a poet to appreciate the mute testimony of the impressive ruins of classical Rome. The Rome of the martyrs, the saints, and the popes meant even more to him as witness to the history of the church's struggle for the cause of Christ. During the course of his stay in the Eternal City he was able to make new friends. While attending an academic convocation held in the Brothers' College of San Giuseppe in the Piazza di Spagna, he met the saintly Brother Leone di Gesu, with whom he kept up correspondence for many years thereafter. He also met for the first time the famous Doctor Rufino Cuervo, a Venezuelan philologist, with whom he had already been corresponding for some time.

As his European pilgrimage was coming to a close, Brother Miguel began to think that it might be possible to realize one of his fondest dreams. He had always wanted to visit the shrine of Our Lady of Lourdes in the hope of finding a cure for his crippled legs. He went so far as to have Doctor Tobar prepare a full medical report on his condition. In the event of a cure, he wanted it verified that the miracle was due to the intercession of his heavenly Mother. This was not to be, however. It proved to be impractical for the returning pilgrims to make the long detour by way of Lourdes. Miguel's disappointment was great but he remained resigned and never complained. The more direct route back through Italy to France took him close to the shrine of Our Lady of Loreto, so at least he had the consolation of a brief stay there. With this he seemed quite content, another sacrifice to offer to his heavenly patroness.

Not long after his return to Quito, Brother Miguel was asked to organize a solemn triduum in thanksgiving for the beatification of John Baptist de La Salle. "Although Rome has provided the most lavish and magnificent celebration of this event," he wrote, "nevertheless Quito, too, can now give proof of its love and commitment to our Institute." The ceremonies were held in the new and spacious chapel of the Beaterio which was officially opened and dedicated as part of the celebration. On three successive days, from August 13 to 15, 1888, pontifical liturgies were celebrated in turn by the bishops of Ibarra, Riobamba and Quito. The most famous preachers available were called upon to extol the virtues and glories of the Blessed Founder of the Brothers. All throughout the triduum, there echoed to the heavens a triumphal hymn composed by Brother Miguel. One of the stanzas follows:

| | |
|---|---|
| *A los pies hollando el oro* | *Trampling underfoot all riches* |
| *Y la pompa mundanal,* | *And the pomp that the world holds dear* |
| *Sólo Dios es su tesoro,* | *God alone is his treasure* |
| *La pobreza su caudal.* | *And poverty the source of his wealth.* |
| *Su descanso es la vigilia,* | *Watching in prayer was his recreation* |
| *Sus delicias padecer,* | *And sufferings his delight.* |
| *Son los pobres su familia,* | *For a family he had only the poor* |
| *La cruz sólo su placer.* | *And the cross alone was his joy.* |

Only a few months later a triduum of a different sort was held in the chapel of the Beaterio. On November 2, thieves broke in and stole two chalices, some patens, and a ciborium filled with consecrated hosts that were ruthlessly tossed aside. The church authorities ordered a triduum of reparation for this act of desecration. For three entire days, from November 7 to 9, the Brothers' community devoted itself to prayer for this intention. Brother Miguel, who always had a special devotion to Jesus in the Blessed Sacrament, was particularly upset. He multiplied his prayers and penances and was seen many times during these days shedding copious tears and prostrating himself on the ground. He took the occasion to publish a leaflet entitled, *A Triduum of Reparation*, by way of expressing publicly his grief at the outrage and his love for Jesus in the Blessed Sacrament. By a strange coincidence, Brother Raphael, the Director of the community, fell ill shortly thereafter and soon died. In the manner of thinking at the time, there were those who interpreted this as a sacrifice demanded of the community by divine justice to make amends for the profanation.

Through all of this, the work of the school and the routine of the religious and community life of the Brothers went on. Despite the demands of his daily classes, his duties as inspector of schools, his role in the public examinations, and the special energy he devoted to preparing his students for their first Holy Communion, Brother Miguel found time to read, to study, and to write for publication. As was customary among the Brothers at the time, his published works did not bear his name but simply the inscription, "By a Brother of the Christian Schools." But there was no secret at all as to the real identity of the author. More and more the rare talent of Brother Miguel began to be recognized and his fame began to spread.

A goodly number of Brother Miguel's published writings were intended for use as texts in the religion classes of the schools. Others took the form of translations of works relating to the Institute to serve as an inspiration for the Brothers. Miguel was also something of a poet but he did not think highly of his talent in this regard. Some of his poetry was composed for public celebrations. Most of his writing in this genre was intended either for his personal friends or as a private vehicle to express his innermost religious feelings.

What most attracted the attention of scholars outside the Institute were his published studies on the Spanish (Castilian) language. That he was no mere hack writer or duplicator of course outlines for student use can be seen from the judgment passed on his publications by competent professionals. In 1890 no less a personage than the Dean of the Faculty of Philosophy and Letters of the University of Ecuador was so impressed with Miguel's *Compendio del curso teórico-práctico de Gramática castellana* that he persuaded the ministry of Education to make it a required text for all the schools in Ecuador.

Similar testimony comes from Doctor Honorato Vásquez. Writing from Madrid in 1910 when, as the Ambassador to Spain from Ecuador, he learned of Brother Miguel's death, he says in part:

> *Always a child at heart, he* [Brother Miguel] *remained devoted to the young, always mindful of the special regard that Our Lord Jesus Christ had for children. . . . And it was this predilection that led him always to use his learned pen in such a way as to have young people in mind. That is why the literary work of Brother Miguel is so admirable. His work was always published anonymously since his humility led him to omit his name from his books, something that ought soon to be rectified.*
>
> *Of all the things that he wrote, I admire nothing quite*

*so much as his books dealing with Castilian Spanish. I do not know anyone writing in Spanish, whether in Spain or in South America, who can rival him in clarity, methodology, precision, ease of expression, and that special attentiveness that understands the workings of the young mind.... The work of Brother Miguel extends from the elementary courses all the way to the most advanced. His material is insightful, scholarly, and full of illustrations. It constitutes a sure guide for the study of the Spanish language.... Brother Miguel has steeped himself in the classics of Spanish literature and everything he writes bears the stamp of its noble origin.*

This last remark provides a clue as to Brother Miguel's own intellectual formation. In the 19th century it was simply unthinkable that Brothers should be allowed to pursue university studies on their own. Yet it remains a fact that here and there throughout the Institute some Brothers, by dint of personal energy and precious moments stolen from time allotted to recreation and sleep, were able to educate themselves to the point of being accepted among the intellectual elite. Such was the case, for example, in the United States with the early professors and presidents of the university colleges that were opened by the Brothers to meet the needs of the immigrant generations. These Brothers were all self-taught but highly respected by their formally trained counterparts in fields as disparate as philosophy, literature, classical languages, mathematics, biology and engineering. So it was with Brother Miguel.

He loved books and was often quoted as saying that a community without books is like a granary without grain. He was well read in the Spanish classics: Teresa of Avila and John of the Cross, Luis of Granada, Cervantes, the classic Spanish poets, and contemporary writers such as Donoso Cortés. He treasured in his room a collection of the principal authorities in the field of linguistics, not only Spanish but French and English as well. In the collection were also some rare volumes devoted to the various South American dialects. These books of his became something like personal friends. Whenever he had the occasion to lend them out he would always say: "Please take good care of them."

Brother Miguel was not entirely self-taught however. In the absence of the opportunities for direction and consultation that a university provides, he developed close ties with some of the best known South American poets, writers and linguists. In his extensive correspondence with them he managed to obtain professional evaluation of his work, new leads to follow in his research, and the occasion to contribute in turn his own discoveries and insights to the general dialogue. Among these contacts, Carlos Tobar, the President of the Academy of Ecuador, Belisario Peña, the Colombian poet, and Rufino Cuervo, the Venezuelan philologist, held a special place in his esteem.

*National Academy of Ecuador, 1892. Standing (l. to r.): Brother Miguel, Roberto Espinosa, Miguel Egas, Carlos R. Tobar, and Quintiliano Sánchez; Seated (l. to r.): Juan León Mera, Luis Cordero, Julio Castro, Pablo Herrera, and José M. Espinosa.*

*"In Brother Miguel we recognize a scholar who, for such a long time and with such distinction, has been engaged in research and publications that have helped to standardize and beautify the language and have brought honor to our country as well."*

The texts of the letters exchanged between Brother Miguel and these men are almost embarrassing in their effusive Latinate style, replete with pious sentiments and expressions of the kind of love the Greeks called *philia*, possible only to persons bound together by a common interest. For example, when Brother Miguel was setting out for Rome, Belisario Peña wrote: "I am writing these lines to tell you that not only will I not forget you but that you are one of the persons I love best in the world." Later on, when Peña was exiled from Ecuador for being too militantly Catholic, Brother Miguel wrote: "How long the days seem when I cannot delight in your presence or even receive news of you. But if we're not united in body, we are at least united in the Heart of Jesus."

In the latter half of the 19th century, an earned doctoral degree was not the only or even the surest guarantee of acceptance among the intellectual elite. It was considered much more prestigious to be elected to one of the national academies, the Académie Française being perhaps the most famous. In 1892, the death of General Salazar left a vacancy in the National Academy of Ecuador, and Brother Miguel was unanimously elected to fill the vacancy. His friend, Doctor Carlos Tobar, who had accompanied him on the trip to Rome, was still President of the Academy. In his letter to Brother Miguel notifying him officially of his election, Doctor Tobar assured him of the great esteem that all the members of the Academy had for him. In him they were recognizing "a scholar who, for such a long time and with such distinction, has been engaged in research and publications that have helped to standardize and beautify the language and have brought honor to our country as well."

When asked for his formal acceptance, Brother Miguel characteristically declared his unworthiness. He agreed to accept only through obedience since his superiors had asked him to do so. When asked what subject he would address in his acceptance speech, Brother Miguel replied: "You know, my friend, that I am nothing more than a simpleton. There is no justification for this honor you have given me. In my wildest dreams I would not have thought of such a thing. However, on the day of my reception, I shall first of all speak words of praise for my predecessor in the academic chair. Then, if my superiors approve, I shall address the question of the influence of Christianity on morality, the arts and the sciences. This topic strikes me as very relevant to our times and needs to be given voice here in the capital where, to its shame, so many anti-religious movements are afoot."

The ceremony was held appropriately enough in the great hall of the Beaterio. The date was August 2, 1892. When the members of the Academy arrived, accompanied by Luis Cordero, the President of the Republic of Ecuador, they were received by the Brothers with great formality. Doctor Tobar replied: "Brothers, this day is yours and it is a great pleasure for us to be here." Then the dignitaries were ushered into the great hall where a large gathering of distinguished guests had already assembled. After the members of the Academy had been seated on the stage, the President declared the session opened. Two members of the Academy were delegated to escort their new colleague to be formally seated in the vacant chair.

When the time came, Brother Miguel delivered his discourse in a voice that rang strong and clear. The address was lengthy by today's standards, running to more than 40 closely printed pages. His introductory remarks in praise of his predecessor were typically humble and unassuming. "Quite simply," he said, "I realize that it is not for me to sing the praises of General Salazar. He, a great military commander, controlled the armies which defend the country; I, a poor and not very well-known schoolteacher, control only a small band of lively youngsters."

In the main body of his address, Brother Miguel traced the history of the influence of Christianity with his usual clarity, originality, breadth of learning and copious illustration. He concluded with a reference to Columbus: "Like him, though lacking his greatness and fame, I have merely succeeded in placing one foot on the shores of a continent which has been known to God alone, who draws us by the riches and captivates us by the more than human beauty of our native land." The entire speech was later published in the Journal of the Academy.

At the conclusion of Brother Miguel's address, Doctor Quintiliano Sánchez, an officer in the Academy, rose in turn to praise the newest member. In his biography of Brother Miguel, Brother Columban Cluderay remarks that it was "a speech which provides us with a contemporary opinion of our hero and at the same time gives an idea of his standing as a scholar and of the reasons for the distinctions conferred upon him." For that reason, it is worth quoting some of the text in the translation that Brother Columban provides:

> *This is today a great occasion for our Academy when we signify the nation's great esteem for the Brothers by receiving as one of our members one of the most distinguished sons of John Baptist de La Salle. It is, I am sure, the first time that a religious clothed in the simple but glorious livery of the apostle of children has been elevated to an academic chair. Though so young, he has the wisdom of one who has grown old in the daily work of the classroom. His pen has enriched our schools with classic education manuals, works which combine clarity and simplicity with perfect method and elegance of language. I must confess that I have always admired Brother Miguel's unaffected candor and I am so thrilled today that this man who always sought to hide his talent and avoid publicity has been officially honored.*
>
> *Further, I am so pleased because no one is worthier to be a member of this Academy, whose work is to maintain the purity and beauty of the Spanish language, than Brother Miguel, for he knows it so well, has studied it so deeply, has become a master of the idiom, which indeed is well illustrated in his own writings. He has revealed its treasures and shown its beauties to innumerable pupils who still flock around him, drawn irresistibly by his virtue and his genius which are both adorned by his wisdom and humility.*
>
> *The Academy has made a just and happy choice in electing our new colleague. Also, in choosing a son of John Baptist de La Salle, we are enhancing the reputation – if that is possible – of an Institute which means so much to us, this body of devoted men whose schools have produced those men of piety and learning who are the boast of our country.*

Membership in the Academy of Ecuador, as in all the famous national academies, was no mere honorary title without further demands beyond the formal ceremony in which it was conferred. The Academy held regular meetings to discuss scholarly topics and sponsored public lectures and literary gatherings of various kinds. Brother Miguel, whose personal preference might have been for the quiet routine of the Brothers' community and school, accepted fully his responsibilities as a member of the Academy and he played an important and constructive part in its activities.

The same Doctor Sánchez who praised him so lavishly at his installation went out of his way to express his personal satisfaction that the expectations of the Academy in electing Brother Miguel had not been disappointed. After Brother Miguel's death in 1910, Doctor Sánchez, at that time still an officer in the Academy, wrote the following: "His good judgment, his learning, and his powerful mind were brilliantly revealed whenever in our meetings we discussed any aspect of literature. For me, his opinion was decisive and all the more agreeable because he expressed it with that modesty and deference which were so natural to him. To me Brother Miguel was as learned as he was holy and as holy as he was learned."

Other academic honors were not long in coming. To begin with, the Academy of Ecuador was affiliated with the Royal Academy of Spain of which Brother Miguel automatically became a corresponding member. Soon thereafter it came to the attention of the academic community in France that Brother Miguel was an outstanding student and devoted advocate of the French language and culture in Ecuador. In 1900, the French Counsul General came to the Beaterio and presented Brother Miguel with the *Palmes académiques* in the name of the French government. Dated May 26, 1900, the diploma of the French Academy is inscribed to "Señor Francisco Febres Cordero, in religion Brother Miguel, Member of the Academy of Ecuador in Quito and Corresponding Member of the Academy of Letters in Madrid." It was signed by G. Leygues, the French Minister of Public Instruction and Fine Arts. Brother Miguel accepted the honor graciously, declaring as usual his unworthiness. One Brother wrote later: "That was the only time we ever saw him wear the decoration. He never again took it from its case, despite the repeated suggestions of the

French Consul that he wear it more often." Then in 1906 he was designated as a corresponding member of the Academy of Venezuela. He never said anything about this to anyone. It was only after his death that the diploma was found among his effects.

# VI. Holiness and Wholeness

In the course of the events narrated thus far, two aspects of Brother Miguel have been given some prominence: his success as a teacher in the classroom and his achievements as a scholar and author. Important as these qualities are, they are not enough in and by themselves to constitute holiness of life, much less that extraordinary kind of holiness that leads to formal canonization. Despite the fact that Brother Miguel's holiness is abundantly clear from his personal diaries and the recollections of those who knew him well, it is not easy to present this aspect of the man in such a way as to make it understandable and attractive to people today.

The early biographers had no such problem, coming as they did from the same spiritual environment. Convinced that a saint had been among them, they described their subject in the manner best calculated to carry weight in the juridical processes leading to canonization. Thus the third Spanish edition of the original French biography devotes three whole chapters covering 60 pages, most of it in fine print, to *El Hermano Miguel en Quito: Virtudes y devociones.*

There are difficulties with this analytic approach, however. It tends to be abstract, a priori, and apologetic, as if holiness could be established by means of a checklist of the supernatural and moral virtues. Thus in the case of Brother Miguel, the biographers begin by gathering evidence to show that he possessed in a high degree each of the theological (or God-directed) virtues in turn. *Faith,* first of all, in terms of his study of religion, his love for Sacred Scripture, his loyalty to the church and its teaching, his respect for priests and the voice of God in his superiors; then *hope,* through his confidence in God's mercy, his desire for salvation, his trust in divine providence during difficult times; finally *charity* seen in his ardent love for God, serving God in others, his piety, his prayer, his devotion to Jesus.

Then evidence is brought to bear on his "human" virtues of goodness and equanimity; his apostolic zeal for souls; his observance of the three vows of religion; his fidelity to the Institute and observance of its Rule; his devotion to St. John Baptist de La Salle; his humility and practices of mortification; his devotion to the Blessed Mother and St. Joseph. Although each of these characteristic "virtues" is abundantly illustrated from Miguel's own writings and stories about him, this approach seems much too artificial. Brother Miguel himself did not compartmentalize his spiritual life in quite that way. He seems to have been much more conscious of the need to integrate his interior life with his external style; he did not isolate his apostolic zeal from his religious faith, nor his love for the Institute from his love for God.

A very different approach might be to trace the course of Brother Miguel's spiritual development from the time he was a child through his mature years up until his death. This might not be as impossible as it seems. He left behind extensive diaries that are dated, as are the external events that served as occasions for his spiritual growth. During the annual retreat that all the Brothers are required to make, he took extensive notes and wrote out all his resolutions, year after year. Quite remarkably, he kept his entire collection of particular examen booklets covering the 40 years of his life as a Brother, almost to the day he died. In these booklets each day he listed the particular defect he was trying to overcome or the virtue he was attempting to acquire.

In the case of Brother Miguel, this rare and precious evidence was made available to the prelates in Barcelona in charge of the preliminary stages in the canonization process. They were understandably astonished to find such a detailed record of the inmost strivings of a saintly spirit. All in all then, there is a great deal available to serve as a basis for a fully documented spiritual biography of Brother Miguel. Fascinating as it might be to trace such a spiritual journey, that kind of study far exceeds the purposes and the readily available resources of this present work. Furthermore, a hasty sampling of the evidence seems to indicate a certain consistency in Brother Miguel's spiritual and devotional life. Although he had his struggles and difficulties and certainly matured along the way, by and large his religious orientation seems to have been in place from the start and to have remained fairly consistent throughout the rest of his life.

The best that can be attempted, then, in this brief survey is to try to capture clues to the holiness of Brother Miguel in the appearance of the man, his habits and his lifestyle together with the impression he made on others. In this light, it might be possible to lift the veil a bit and look into some few of his own writings to get a glimpse at least of the salient features of his personal share in the holiness of God.

His first biographer, writing in French, gives this description of the physical appearance of Brother Miguel:

*Our beloved Ecuadorian Brother was certainly not gifted by heaven with that sort of plastic beauty which so easily fades with the years. Although rather tall in stature, his posture became stooped quite early in his life. His countenance was dark and somewhat emaciated, prematurely furrowed with wrinkles that came from his sufferings and his practices of mortification. Even so, his facial expression reflected in some indefinable way the beauty of his soul and the interior illumination of divine grace. This reverberated through his whole being which overflowed with a certain gentleness that came from his peaceful and kindly nature. His very thin lips always bore the glimmer of a continual and gracious smile. His eyes, limpid and transparent as those of the most innocent child, sparkled with the joy and serenity that could only be due to that indescribable peace of which Scripture speaks. In sum, the serene expression in all his features gave the impression that underneath there was a calm and imperturbable spirit.*

The striking photographs and the portrait that we have of Brother Miguel provide some evidence that this description is accurate.

As far as his lifestyle is concerned, all that needs be said is that Brother Miguel was meticulous in the observance of every detail of the traditional Rule of the Brothers that had been handed down from the time of John Baptist de La Salle almost two centuries earlier. Only recently abrogated and replaced as part of the adaptation and renewal called for by Vatican Council II, this traditional Rule set uniform standards for the community and religious life of all the Brothers throughout the world. The older generations of Brothers still living would have been required to live this Rule to the letter in their novitiate days. For many Brothers, adaptations had to be made later on in community, especially in English-speaking countries, to meet changes of time and culture as well as the demands of the apostolate. Such adaptations were not so common among the French communities in the 19th century, a policy that the French Brothers brought with them to new foundations in other Catholic countries including, for example, Ecuador. For Brother Miguel, therefore, the strict observance of the Brothers' Rule was not merely a passing phase of his formation in the novitiate but a norm to be followed for the rest of his days.

What did this mean concretely on a day-to-day basis? The religious habit was worn in private and in public from the time of rising in the morning until going to bed at night. The regularly scheduled religious exercises were followed day in and day out, including weekends and holidays, and special permission was required when it was necessary to be absent, as must have happened frequently with Brother Miguel. Each Brother was expected to kneel down to adore God present upon entering or leaving any room in the house, and it is reported that Brother Miguel did this with special fervor.

As an exercise in humiliation, the Brothers accused themselves publicly of their faults every day and accused one another once a week. Self-imposed penances such as kneeling out in chapel with arms extended or taking meals on one's knees were common. Permission had to be sought for the slightest expenditures or any physical necessities, while external signs of respect and childlike dependence on superiors were taken for granted, quite independently of the age, maturity, or talents of any particular Brother. The Rosary was recited while walking through the streets; social contacts even with the parents of the students were severely restricted. Despite his superior intelligence, his productive scholarship, and his wide fame, the evidence is that Brother Miguel kept up all these observances in the manner of the most dedicated novice in the first fervor and isolation of his novitiate year. But with him it lasted a lifetime.

Even so, this exemplary observance does not in itself constitute sanctity. Probably most of the Brothers in Ecuador at that time conformed more or less to the same pattern of religious life. It was something taken for granted. Besides, there have been other Brothers before and since in many parts of the Institute who were as exacting as Brother Miguel in the observance of the traditional Rule. Yet not all of them, very few in fact, were instinctively recognized by their confreres as saints. In some cases, the traces of compulsive or other eccentric behavioral patterns made such Brothers very disagreeable to live with. One wise old Brother once remarked: "To live with the saints in heaven is a joy and a glory; to live with a 'saint' on earth is quite another story." Such was decidedly not the case with Brother Miguel. The Brothers he lived with liked him, they liked to be with him, they appreciated his talents, they admired his modesty in not flaunting his achievements, they knew he was a saint.

As with his physiognomy, his external observance of the Rule was transformed into something radiant and beautiful by the deep religious spirit that lay beneath it. This comes through very clearly in the reminiscences of the Brothers who shared community with him. "In 1870 when I arrived in Quito," one Brother wrote, "everybody already thought of young Miguel as a saint. He was considered the treasure of the community. From that time on, our opinion of him never changed a bit." One Brother Provincial put it his way: "From the moment he came to the Beaterio, his virtue was outstanding and appreciated by everybody. He very rapidly acquired the reputation of being a saint. I have known him well for 16 years and that has always been my own personal opinion of him."

Finally, a Brother who taught in the schools of Quito for more than 40 years had this to say: "Our students, their parents, and our friends used to vie with one another in proclaiming 'Brother Miguel is a saint.' For myself, I declare that I have never seen a Brother so holy, so faithful to the Rule, so recollected. . . . Whatever may be said in praise of his virtue, no matter how lofty the claims, there is no possibility of exaggeration in his case." There is reason, therefore, to suppose that the sanctity of Brother Miguel would have emerged no matter what the external style of religious life, including that of today where greater freedom, diversity and personal responsibility make rather different, but no less challenging, demands on those who would live out their Christian commitment in this way.

In order to penetrate to the source of the sanctity of Brother Miguel, it is necessary to go beyond the externals and to seek in his private notes and personal reflections the very center of his entire being. And there the secret is revealed: he was in love with God. Not in some abstract way. To him God was real, a living presence, the personal object of his affection and adoration, available to his every waking thought. It almost seems like an invasion of privacy to read expressions such as these: *Dios mío, ¡os amo! ¡Oh Dios mío, Vos que tanto me amáis, os amo yo también! ¡Cúanto os amo!* And to any true lover, the prospect of offending the beloved is unthinkable. On one occasion he literally wrote in his own blood: "I consider it a thousand times better, my gentle Jesus, to die loving you than to live offending you. You will be the God of my heart and my inheritance for all eternity. I would rather die a thousand times than be unfaithful. Every fiber of my heart has only one desire, Lord, and that is never to cease belonging to you." It is doubtful that Brother Miguel ever thought of the love of God as a "commandment," not even the first and the summation of all the others. He knew, in biblical terms, that "God is love." That was all he needed to feel humbled by the grace-given opportunity to respond in kind.

This love for God was personalized in a special way by his lively devotion to God incarnate in Jesus Christ. The Sacred Heart of Jesus was a particularly appropriate symbol for Brother Miguel as an expression of God's love for him and a way to personalize his own response of love. He was devoted also to the Infant Jesus to whom he often entrusted the needs of his young charges and the care of their souls. His sense of the presence of Jesus in the Blessed Sacrament was so real and well-nigh physical as to verge on the outer limits of sound theology. This relationship of intimacy with Jesus extended naturally to his Blessed Mother Mary and to St. Joseph. With childlike confidence and simplicity, Brother Miguel would address them frequently as if they were in a face-to-face conversation. He even wrote letters to them which he dated and signed. Every year he wrote a letter to St. Joseph on March 18, the eve of his feast day, praising the Saint's virtues and asking for favors for himself and for others. In the letter to St. Joseph dated March 18, 1877, he included 11 petitions for his own spiritual needs, eight for the Institute, five for his family, eight for his students and seven for the church. One is tempted to wonder what he might have done with the present practice of offering such petitions in the context of the liturgy.

But it was to Mary, the Mother of Jesus and his own heavenly Mother, that Brother Miguel expressed himself with all the filial ardor of his poetic and devoted soul. Here is an act of consecration he addressed to her:

*May 31, 1875*

*My dearest Mamita, you know very well that I am a poor little nobody and that there is nothing in me worthy of presenting before your holy altar. I do not have those virtues that are represented by the purity of the lily, the humility of the violet and the graciousness of the rose. Nothing remains in me except a heart that is dried up and worn down with countless sins and tyrannical passions. If you will, then, receive this offering, not because the one who makes it is of any worth, but in view of the anguish with which it is made. I give you my whole heart without reserve in the hope that you will purify it and keep it as your own, securely locked, as it were, among your precious jewels, so that I would never dare to take it back to hand over to the archenemy of souls.*

[Signed] *Brother Miguel*


On one of his annual retreats, Miguel took a resolution to dedicate each day to his heavenly Mother in a special way, by honoring on Sunday her virginal purity, on Monday her love of God, on Tuesday her love of neighbor, on Wednesday her spirit of silence and recollection, on Thursday her indifference toward earthly things, on Friday her love of Jesus crucified, and on Saturday her deep humility.

Dramatic and personal as was Brother Miguel's intense love for God and his intimate relationship to Jesus, Mary and Joseph, this never led him along the path of an otherworldly and disembodied mysticism. For him, the love of God was not an abstraction, neither was his love for the neighbor. His love extended generously to the living persons who were his students, his Brothers, and his professional colleagues. In Lasallian terms, his was an apostolic spirituality. Concerning his vocation, he wrote:

*In the miserable state of modern society, my divine Savior calls me to conquer souls, without really needing my help or without considering my absolute incapacity for any good. Can I be deaf to his voice? Can I be afraid of disappointment when he promises to be with me? Can I be so bold as to refuse this demonstration of love and gratitude?*

*I must engage in all the works that I undertake with a spirit of love, of gratitude for the divine goodness which has been gracious enough to employ me for his glory and the salvation of souls.*

Then there is this touching example of Miguel "trying to use his influence" for the good of his students:

*Jesus, Mary, and Joseph: All the children that come here belong to you. That is why I ask you to guard and protect them in every way. Impart to them a great horror of sin and a holy fear of offending you. God grant that they may always be devout and put into practice all that I teach them.*

*Jesus, Mary and Joseph, don't allow it to happen that they offend you or suffer the disgrace of staining their souls so precious in your eyes. I am not worthy that you should grant me these favors. But since you have confided these children to my care, I hope that you will supply for my deficiencies.*

*I am, your humble and unworthy servant,*

*[Signed] Brother Miguel*

"*What a marvelous thing it is, that God has called me to this holy vocation.*"

Finally, he composed this prayer which he would say on the way to class:

*Divine Heart of Jesus, preserve me from all sin and do not allow it to happen that I should be an occasion of scandal for any of these children that you love so much. . . . They are little angels. Do not allow me, through my bad example and my defects, to change them into the devils who are your enemies. No, Never! I would rather die a thousand times, my Jesus, rather than let that happen.*

In all of this it is clear that Brother Miguel considered his intimacy with God and his heavenly patrons as a gift given, not just for himself, but for the benefit of those entrusted to his care.

Granted that the holiness of Brother Miguel was rooted in the love of God and overflowed into an active apostolate and zeal for souls, there is yet a third element that shines through it all. He was a first-rate human being, a fundamentally good person, cheerful, kindly toward others, willing to be of service and happy in whatever he was called upon to do. Not all the saints have had the same ability to let the sunshine in, to radiate peace, to appear as messengers who bring tidings of great joy. Yet this is a recurrent theme in the reminiscences of all those who lived with Brother Miguel. It comes through as well in his own writings. "What a marvelous thing it is," he wrote, "that God has called me to this holy vocation." He encouraged others to have the same optimism. "Our first reaction in dealing with others," he said on another occasion, "should always be to find something about them worthy of praise." In short he made sanctity seem easy and attractive.

For him personally, however, it wasn't all sweetness and light. Brother Miguel had his problems as everyone does. The determination to keep in balance his spiritual sensitivity, the demands of the apostolate, and a cheerful attitude in his human relationships was a continual struggle. His poor physical health and his crippled legs did not make the ascent to the heights of sanctity any easier. The state of his soul was every bit as much a concern for him as the miserable condition of his body. So intense and personal was his love for God that even the slightest moral fault seemed to him like a betrayal. His conciousness of having failed to respond fully to what he thought God required of him caused him mental and emotional torment. There is evidence in his writings that he had often to combat the demand of the sexual urge, normal in every maturing and mature male, but which he scarcely understood and inevitably interpreted in the light of the negative attitude toward the body and its sexual functions so prevalent in the religious climate of the time. Although he fully accepted the principle that meditation or mental prayer is an essential support of the religious life, it seems that he found this exercise difficult. Vocal prayer or the written prayers that he composed were much more congenial to him than the formal process outlined in the method of mental prayer traditional among the Brothers. He often prayed to St. Joseph to help him master the technique. It is also clear from his writings that, at least in his own view, he had to fight the temptation to take pride in his work, the success that he had, and the praises heaped upon him. In addition to all these interior trials, there were the inevitable problems of community living: capricious superiors, suspicious or jealous confreres, his importunate friends who thought little of interrupting his work or his devotions to seek his counsel and assistance.

It must also be said that not everything in Brother Miguel was beyond criticism, certainly not in the perspective of history. He was not in every respect a man for all seasons or a saint for all times. For one thing, the style of religious life that he lived in slavish obedience to the Rule and superiors has all but disappeared in apostolic religious institutes. Although his love for God and the saints was undoubtedly genuine, his theological concepts were decidedly naive, derived for the most part from the formulas of the catechism made concrete in the vivid religious imagination of his childhood. In particular his understanding of sin and salvation would, by today's standards, be judged to be rather narrow.

The same is true of his conservative political stance based on the traditional doctrine of the union of church and state. His love for the Founder and the Institute led him to an excessive enthusiasm for everything French despite the fact that, as a native Ecuadorian, he might have been expected to be somewhat more alert to the colonialist implications of such an attitude. His extensive research into the origins and structure of the Castilian Spanish language led him into the trap of linguistic classicism. He seems to have had little theoretical regard for language as an historical and dynamic reality. All of this says nothing more than that he was a man of his times. As such he should not be judged by the standards and insights of a subsequent time or another quite different cultural milieu.

When all is said and done the fact remains that Brother Miguel was and is a saint. The point was made in the opening chapter of this brief survey that sanctity consists not so much in what one does – although in the case of Brother Miguel that was considerable – but in what a person is, in the deepest self, and before God. From that point of view, the final word that has to be said about this man's holiness is his personal wholeness. In contemporary lingo, he had his act together. Or to put it another way, he knew who he was. Ardent lover of God, devoted son to his heavenly Mother, he was yet an effective teacher, a productive scholar, and a cheerful person to be with. These varied facets of his self-identity interpenetrated and drew strength, the one from the other. The saint that he was and was recognized to be, the evident share that he had in the holiness of God, were the source and the principle of this personal integrity in all that he did.

For that reason Brother Miguel is for Christians – and especially for Christian Brothers – of every time and every place a hero to celebrate and a model to imitate. Pope Paul VI, in the homily he delivered on the occasion of the beatification ceremony in 1977, expressed it in these words: "If we ask ourselves the basic reason for such human and religious fruitfulness, for that success in his exemplary task as a catechist, we find it in the depths of his rich spirit, which led him to become wisdom clothed in love, science that sees the human being in the light of Christ, a divine image that is projected. . . . towards eternal horizons. This is the great secret, the key to the success won by Brother Miguel, the sublime realization of a great ideal and for that reason a hero for our time."

# VII. New Responsibilities

From the time Brother Miguel began his teaching career in 1869 the school at the Beaterio had provided the setting for his life and work. The fortunes of the school were inextricably linked to his own. Over the years the school had prospered. By the year 1890 the superior classes had attained the status, if not the name, of a normal school or training college for teachers, awarding diplomas that granted the right to teach to those who passed the rather rigorous qualifying examinations.

At about the same time an evening school was opened for working adults who wanted to complete their education. Out of these developments was formed the De La Salle Institute which became independent in 1894 and was moved, providentially as it turned out, to a new location in the Cebollar district close to the Brothers' novitiate. Intended to serve the need for a more advanced education among the well-to-do and to provide boarding facilities as well, the new Institute was inaugurated amid great ceremony with the President of the Republic, Luis Cordero, presiding. Brother Miguel was assigned to teach the advanced classes in Spanish grammar and literature and also to serve as the supervisor of the boarding students. With 1,300 students enrolled in the Beaterio proper, and the opening of the advanced Institute in the Cebollar, the future of the Brothers in Quito looked bright indeed.

But trouble was on the horizon. During holy week of 1895, a decisive confrontation that split the conservative party brought about the resignation of President Luis Cordero. The radical forces in the country took advantage of the division in the dominantly Catholic conservative party and on June 5 a revolution broke out in Guayaquil. General Eloy Alfaro, who had been recalled from exile in Panama, was proclaimed as Supreme Head of the Republic and Commander in Chief of the

Army. The rebel forces successfully defeated the government troops and by August had established themselves in power in Quito.

Early in September, in an attempt to win favor with the new authorities who were flushed with victory and revolutionary zeal, Señor Suárez, the professor of music at the Beaterio, on his own initiative assembled the school choir to sing the revolutionary hymn as part of the ceremonies marking the takeover of the new government. General Alfaro, who had proclaimed from the start, "I come to destroy theocracy in Ecuador!" was pleased by this gesture. He was anxious to win the support of the people and realized that such religiously sponsored events would help to solidify his triumph and his authority. So for a short time the Brothers were left in peace. But as the conservative forces regrouped themselves in nearby Colombia and pockets of resistance developed here and there, the government began to take retaliatory measures against individual citizens, certain bishops and priests, and the Catholic newspapers that were considered hostile.

Just before the start of the new school year the Brothers approached the authorities to ask for the regular stipend that the government provided for the schools and for the necessary guarantees that would allow them to continue teaching. General Alfaro himself was quite agreeable and assured the Brothers that they had nothing to fear. But the very next day he publicly attacked the Archbishop who was known to be friendly to the Brothers. During the next several months the tension and uncertainty of the deteriorating situation made the Provincial, Brother Bernon-Marie, and many other Brothers very nervous. Brothers in temporary vows were allowed to leave the Institute, while many families withdrew their sons from the novitiate. As a result three schools in the outlying towns had to be closed for lack of personnel.

In Quito the new school year began as usual without incident. On October 1, General Alfaro, accompanied by three aides, visited the Beaterio, addressed the student body in glowing terms, ordered some repairs to the buildings, and paid the Brothers the monthly stipend for September. Brother Miguel meanwhile continued with his advanced classes at the De La

Salle Institute in the Cebollar, calm as always, finding a source of confidence for himself and for others in the conviction that the will of God would prevail.

For the next three months General Alfaro was away from Quito. Meanwhile a new opposition movement was being organized in Guayaquil. To strengthen the position of the ruling party in the capital, Alfaro's aides began to organize new triumphal demonstrations in his support. Again the choir of the Beaterio was asked to participate. This time Señor Suárez, the music professor, met with resistance of a different kind. The students, many of whom had lost relatives in the fight against the revolution, simply refused to sing the anthem entitled, *La Libertad*, that the all too accommodating professor had composed for the occasion. The Director of the school, Brother Imonis, sided with the students and wrote to the authorities: "I cannot in conscience accede to what has been asked, or force my students to welcome with triumphal hymns a leader whose stated political platform is to destroy theocracy in Ecuador." This incident led to increasing harassment of the Brothers, and it soon became evident that a showdown was inevitable.

The expected blow was not long in coming. On the following January 28, Brother Bernon-Marie, the Provincial, was summoned to appear before General Alfaro who informed him that the Christian Schools would no longer receive any financial subsidy from the government. The Provincial replied that if such were to be the case, then he needed only time for the Brothers to return to their communities, close the schools and leave the country. The General said that such a move was not necessary, that the Brothers could continue to hold classes and that there was no reason for them to leave the country. The Provincial pointed out, in reply, that this action was in violation of the contract made with the government in 1862, that it effectively deprived the Brothers of their only means of livelihood without which they could not possibly continue.

Accordingly, the Provincial ordered the Brothers' schools in Quito to be closed. When the students arrived at the Beaterio the next day, they found the doors locked and guarded by the police, with the Brothers nowhere to be seen. With the Brothers gone, the only way that the Beaterio was able to continue was for the Archbishop to take over the school and keep it going with the help of some young priests and lay volunteers. The Brothers in their turn decided to start classes in the building in the Cebollar. The De La Salle Institute, with its advanced courses for those who could pay, remained closed. In its place the Brothers opened on March 19, 1896, a new gratuitous school for the poor, named La Sagrada Familia. It was to be maintained by the financial support of the archdiocese and the contributed services of the Brothers.

During this difficult period, overtures were made to Brother Miguel suggesting that important posts in the government schools would be available to him personally if he would be interested. This suggestion that he might be willing to isolate his own case from that of his confreres thoroughly disgusted Brother Miguel. It horrified him to think that anyone would imagine that he would cooperate in such a venture. His indignation and repudiation of the very idea were forceful enough so that no further insinuations of this kind were ever made again.

With the opening of the school at the Sagrada Familia, Brother Miguel returned to the routine of his teaching apostolate at the elementary level with renewed vigor. He was particularly happy to be busy once again preparing the youngsters for their first Holy Communion. Grateful to his holy patrons, Jesus, Mary and Joseph, he composed a poem of thanksgiving in honor of the Holy Family. Meanwhile, students flocked once again in great numbers to this newest Brothers' school. Whereas there had been 1,156 pupils at the Beaterio in 1895, by December, 1896, there were 1,194 enrolled at the Sagrada Familia in El Cebollar.

It was evident, nevertheless, that the troubles of 1895 and 1896 did irreparable harm to the Brothers' enterprises throughout Ecuador. Many Brothers fled the country altogether, some going home to France, others to Colombia or Chile. To make up for these losses, it became urgent to reorganize the novitiate, to restore morale, and to make the life of the Brother seem as attractive as possible to young Ecuadorians. For this purpose, the superiors appointed Brother Miguel as Director of Novices, a post he held whenever there were any novices during three distinct periods between 1896 and 1905.

The choice was applauded by everyone but Miguel himself who is reported to have said: "It is very risky to ask someone like myself to take charge of the delicate mission of forming young Brothers when I myself need direction more than anyone." Yet the reports from his novices indicate that he was quite successful in this role. He was patient with their faults but he did not hesitate to send away those he considered unsuitable for the Brothers' life. "The Brothers in Ecuador have to endure many hardships," he wrote, "and so it is important to prepare Brothers who are courageous and who will be proof against any trial." His conferences to the novices were much like his classes: well-organized, clear and to the point, simple in expression, and full of good practical advice. He inculcated in his novices his own love of prayer and his enthusiasm for the Institute, the Founder, and his own vocation. During recreation periods he could be jovial and expansive. When the novices took their long walks to their summerhouse in the country, he would follow on horseback, content to leave his youthful charges in the care of another Brother.

In October, 1902, Brother Miguel was appointed Director of the Sagrada Familia. By that time the school had more than 1,000 students and a community of 22 Brothers. Again, Miguel protested: "I am only a miserable scribe with no administrative ability." Despite his misgivings and the discomfort he felt presiding at the head of the community, he seems to have succeeded at the task. He supervised the discipline in the school and the regular observance of the community in such a way that no one seemed to take offense. One Brother remarked that he gave his orders as if he were asking a favor.

It is a bit surprising, then, that after only ten months as Director he was relieved of the office. The reasons have never been made clear. It may be that the superiors came to agree with his estimate of himself and recognized that he was not in his best element in a position of authority. Or it may be that word had already filtered down that his special talents were needed for far-reaching responsibilities elsewhere. In any case, it was back to teaching as usual, for the time being at least. The Brother who succeeded him as Director of the community wrote this: "As soon as I was appointed his successor, everyone was greatly edified to see Brother Miguel, although the senior member of the community and only recently its superior, giving such respectful submission to this newcomer who had been appointed to direct the community in the name of God. Among the Brothers he was the most deferential, the most humble, and the most trustful of all."

At this time, shortly after the turn of the century, affairs were reaching a critical phase at the center of the Institute in France. The anti-clerical movement was at its height, the Catholic teaching congregations once again among the principal targets. In 1904 came the definitive decree suppressing all teaching congregations in France. The Brothers were given the choice of leaving the Institute or leaving the country. Many of them opted to live out their vocation in various parts of the world, with a significant number going to Spain and Latin America. As early as 1905, Brother Miguel had been alerted to the possibility that he might be called to Europe to translate into Spanish the texts used by the Brothers in the French schools, so that they might more easily adjust to a new educational environment. On April 17, 1905, Brother Miguel wrote to the Assistant Superior General: "My Most Reverend Brother Assistant: Since you have indicated to me on two occasions that I might be called to Europe, I want you to know that I am entirely at your command. . . . I place myself completely in the hands of God for him to dispose of me as he will. This I do in virtue of the vow of obedience and I do it without seeking or refusing anything." When word of all this reached the Brothers in Quito, they did all that they could over the next two years to keep at home their most effective catechist and the best loved Brother in the province.

In March of 1907 Brother Viventien-Aimé, the Assistant Superior General, made his official visit to Ecuador. He asked Brother Miguel whether he was prepared to accompany him to ·Lembecq-lez-Hal, Belgium, promising that after four or five years he would be able to return to Ecuador. Brother Miguel replied: "I want only to do what you command me. As far as I am concerned, it is all the same whether I remain here or whether I go. You decide. I am at your disposal. In that way I will be sure to be doing what God wants." There was great consternation among the Brothers in Quito when they heard the news. The Brother Assistant tried to diffuse their protests with the promise that their beloved confrere would be returning within a few years. An early departure date was set, since the Brother Assistant was expected home for the opening of the new motherhouse at Lembecq, where it had been moved after the expulsion from Paris. The two Brothers left Quito on March 10 amidst great lamentation. Pressed by the Brothers for some souvenir, Brother Miguel finally relented after obtaining permission to distribute among them some holy pictures he had saved. "Thank God," one of them said, "that at least we have a relic of Brother Miguel." Their instincts proved to be correct; they were never to see him again.

The journey took the usual route down the mountains to the port city of Guayaquil, thence to Panama, overland across the isthmus to Colón, by sea to New York, and from there to France. At Guayaquil, where his parents had spent their last years, Brother Miguel was able to make one of his rare, and what would turn out to be the last, contacts with his family. His father had died in 1882 in circumstances that have already been described. Miguel's mother and his brother, Aurelio, died within a year of each other in 1897 and 1898. Of that coincidence Brother Miguel had written:

*Of the many graces which the Lord has been good enough to bestow on my family, one of the greatest, for which I bless, thank and adore his divine Providence, has been the death of my brother which occurred on December 18, 1897, since in that way he was preserved from the many dangers that the world offers in these days of disorder and confusion. Likewise, I thank God for my good and holy mother, who died on November 18, 1898. I pray God that he will reward her for all her virtues since she had her probation during life with so many anxieties and sufferings.*

While Brother Miguel was in Guayaquil in 1907 on his way to Europe, he took advantage of the opportunity to pray at the graves of his father, his mother and his brother. But he made no move to visit his relatives still living there, not even his sister, Anita, whom he dearly loved. Since Miguel never spoke of his family, the Brother Assistant who was traveling with him had no idea that he had a sister living nearby. However, the Superior of the Lazarist Fathers, who knew Anita from her volunteer work with the victims of yellow fever, brought this to the attention of Brother Assistant who then, edified no doubt by this spirit of detachment and resignation, ordered Brother Miguel to go to see his sister and their relatives before embarking for Panama.

On the long and tedious journey to Europe, stopovers were frequently necessary to make connections between land and sea. One of the more interesting of these was the layover for two days in New York. As a first-time visitor to the city, everything about New York caught Miguel's attention, especially the elevated trains, the skyscrapers and the crowds in the streets. But more than anything, he was impressed, as he said, by "the piety of the Catholics of the city and the determination and generosity with which they support the Catholic schools." In one of his letters, Brother Miguel writes how impressed he was by the regard that the church authorities had for the Brothers. He tells the story of the funeral of one of the Brothers that was attended by the Archbishop of New York who arrived unexpectedly and personally presided over the rite of final commendation. When the Brothers offered their thanks for such graciousness, the prelate replied: "That is the least I could do for the Brothers. All of them are precious to me for the help that they give to the clergy of my archdiocese."

At first reading of this letter, it might seem that Brother Miguel was actually present for that occasion. Since the records show that no Brother was buried in New York during the time of his visit, it is more likely that this was an oft-repeated story that Brother Miguel picked up in conversation with the New York Brothers. Impressed as Brother Miguel may have been with New York, the Brothers in New York were evidently impressed with him. After only two days in New York, as Miguel was taking his leave, the Brother Provincial of New York said to his companions: "That Brother is a saint." On April 3, 1907, Brother Miguel and Brother Viventien, Assistant, set sail from New York for Le Havre on the *Lorraine*. They arrived in Paris on April 11, just one month after their departure from Quito.

# VIII. Displacement

At an earlier time in his life, when his family was doing its best to wean him away from his vocation to the Institute of De La Salle, Brother Miguel was sent for a time to the seminary where he described himself as a fish out of water. He might have used the same metaphor – although he did not – to describe his situation in Europe during the years when he lived successively in France, Belgium and Spain, from 1907 until his death in 1910.

The very day after his arrival in Paris on April 12, 1907, Brother Miguel was seized with a frightful fever, caught perhaps during his stay in the fever-ridden port of Guayaquil, and had to take to his bed. The infirmarian of the Brothers has provided the usual testimony to the prompt obedience of Brother Miguel, his total resignation to the will of God, and his fidelity to the religious exercises during an illness that lasted for more than two weeks. In the course of his convalescence he had a close brush with death as the infirmarian told the story:

> One night, during his convalescence, I had suggested that he [Brother Miguel] retire early. He obeyed at once. There was no special reason for me to visit him after night prayer, but something told me that I ought to go look in on him. He was asleep in his room which by then was filled with the smell of illuminating gas. By mistake he had opened the valve, thinking he had closed it. I got there just in time to save our beloved Ecuadorian from almost certain death. Once I got the window open to allow fresh air to circulate through the door, there was time to thank God for having saved him from such a peril to his life.

In due time the health of Brother Miguel began to be restored. After brief pilgrimages to the Basilica of the Sacred Heart at Montmartre and the Shrine of Our Lady of Victories, he set earnestly to work at the Brothers' house on the Rue de Sèvres, Number 78, which had been turned into a sort of publication center and printing establishment. By this device the Brothers were able to maintain a center in Paris just behind the former motherhouse on the Rue Oudinot despite the suppression of religious orders in France three years before. The traditional

*Brother Miguel was occupied totally in the tedious work of translating French textbooks into Spanish and then overseeing the various stages of publication.*

community life went on behind closed doors and, as always, Brother Miguel was a model of devotion, regularity and hard work. One Brother said of him that the only two places where he could ever be found were at his desk in his office and in the chapel.

Brother Miguel was occupied totally in the tedious work of translating French textbooks into Spanish and then overseeing the various stages of publication. He found no time to pursue his own scholarly and aesthetic interests. When works of this kind came from his colleagues in the Academy of Ecuador, he barely skimmed the pages. In short, he turned himself into something of a workhorse, happy in the conviction that this was what God wanted him to do. He also had to contend with those who disagreed with his linguistic theories. One French Brother, with only two or three years of experience with the Spanish language in Latin America, was particularly obnoxious, constantly challenging aspects of Miguel's work. Miguel remained aloof from the controversy, confiding to one Brother: "I don't take part in that kind of argument where each opposing party puts forth his own ideas but the truth suffers in the long run."

Brother Miguel wrote regularly to the Brother Director in Quito to share his impressions of his rare excursions into the city of Paris. One of the things that impressed Miguel the most was how the Brothers in Paris, deprived of their schools, had managed to keep in touch with their former students in an organized way so as to encourage them to persevere in the faith. This undertaking was known as the Society of St. Benedict Joseph Labre. After attending one of the meetings, Brother Miguel wrote on July 22, 1907, to the Director in Quito as follows:

*On Sunday, July 1, I had the good fortune to go to the Basilica of the Sacred Heart at Montmartre and there to assist at a general convocation of "Operation Perseverance." Something like a thousand young men gathered together under those stark domes of the Basilica for Mass and the majority of them received Holy Communion.*

*A few days later, that is on July 14, the national holiday, and also on the free day following on the 15th, more than*

*one hundred young men came to Athis to make a spiritual*
*retreat while their friends were enjoying the holiday and*
*taking it easy. This group of retreatants was really*
*something beautiful to see!*

In a lighter vein, the Brothers in the community at Rue de
Sèvres kept pressuring Brother Miguel, saying that no
Ecuadorian who had lived in Paris should be allowed to depart
until he had visited the Ark of Noah. There in the Bois de
Boulogne in the Jardin des Plantes one could see a magnificent
collection of all the animals "saved by God from the flood."
"You've just got to see it," they insisted. So Miguel finally went
and after his visit he wrote this description back to Quito:

*In order to take a brief respite and to give my tired brain*
*a rest, these good Brothers here force me every once in a*
*while to throw caution to the winds and let them show me*
*some of the famous attractions in this fabulous capital of*
*theirs. There is in the Jardin des Plantes a veritable Ark*
*of Noah containing living examples of the most varied spe-*
*cies of animals, birds, and reptiles. Without fear of exag-*
*geration and without any flight of rhetorical fancy, I can*
*say that all the lands of the earth, all the mountains of the*
*globe, all the oceans and all the climatic zones, are*
*represented in these huge enclosures, these oddly shaped*
*pools, these fancy bird cages. The Parisians, and even more*
*so the tourists, come here to this little corner of modern*
*Babylon where they can contemplate the whole universe.*
*There are lions, tigers, and zebras from Africa; elephants,*
*panthers, and camels from Asia. By contrast there is only*
*our humble llama from Ecuador. . . . but above them all fly*
*the eagles and the condor of our American Andes.*

There is a bit of naiveté, chauvinism, and homesickness, all in
one letter, but charming all the same.

In the same vein, it is clear how much Brother Miguel missed
his friends among the Brothers in Ecuador and his work with
the first Holy Communion classes. He wrote to Quito on May
16, 1907:

*Your letter, dear Brother Director, has caused me great*

*concern but it allows me to share in the sickness of one of our Brothers and the sorrow that it has brought to all of you. I only hope that the Lord will give to you all the strength and courage to sanctify this bitter trial and transform it into a source of spiritual benefit.*

*I have not lost sight, no, not even for a day, of our beloved youngsters who are preparing for their first Holy Communion. I have recommended them in my prayers to the Divine Child Jesus and to the Most Holy Virgin, and not only them but all the Brothers engaged in preparing them for this great event. My heart is always with them, but above all on that happy day when for the first time they will be allowed to share in the heavenly banquet.*

Another clue as to Miguel's sense of separation or homesickness, if one could call it that, is this letter that he wrote to a sick confrere in Quito on June 29, 1907:

*I hear that the burden of too much work has finally laid you low and that you are ill. How I wish I could help in some way to relieve your suffering! But what better source of help and relief can there be than the Divine Jesus and his Most Holy Mother for whom you have sacrificed your very self? Have courage, then, my very dear Brother. The Lord our God is a very generous paymaster. My heart and my thoughts are never very far away from all of you. Many times I have given full rein to my sighs and tears, but only God has witnessed them. I say this only to assure you that I do not think that our separation and the distance between us have in any way erased from my memory the remembrance of all my friends.*

It is possible to imagine, with this rather untypical admission to "sighs and tears," how much it must have cost Brother Miguel to find in the acceptance of God's will the strength to maintain peace in his heart, perseverance in his work, and serenity in his relationships in a community so far away from home.

Some relief from the boring routine at Rue de Sèvres came in July of 1907 when Brother Miguel was transferred to the motherhouse of the Institute at Lembecq-lez-Hal, a suburb of

Brussels in Belgium. The property was extensive in a sylvan setting with massive and multiple buildings, open courtyards, gardens and parks, and in every way a contrast to the urban environment, the hustle and bustle that surrounded the house on the Rue de Sèvres.

Located at Lembecq were the central administrative offices of the Institute, recently moved from Paris, a junior novitiate for very young candidates, and a scholasticate or training college for young Brothers about to enter the classroom – a recent innovation in Institute policy. This complex administrative structure provided Brother Miguel with occasional and challenging breaks from the solitary work of translation since he would often be called upon to replace a Brother, especially in the Spanish or religion classes, as a vacancy in one or another of the departments would require. Besides, the composition of these various inter-related communities provided an international mix of Brothers from all over the world that could not be other than stimulating for a man of Brother Miguel's interests and attainments. Among those whom he met in this way was Brother Paul Joseph who was to become the first to write a biography of Brother Miguel.

When Brother Miguel arrived in Lembecq it was summer. The gardens were in full bloom and the weather was ideal. Brother Miguel's health was never better, and his sensitive spirit was responsive to the beauties of nature all around him. But with the coming of autumn he began to suffer again from the attacks of recurrent fever which, as he used to say jokingly, he should have taken out of his baggage and left behind at Guayaquil. During the following winter he suffered a great deal. Not that the winters in Belgium are all that severe. But most of the time the sky is overcast, the sun rises late, sets early and is hardly ever seen. There is constant fog and drizzle, the wind is damp and penetrating, and, in short, the long gray winter seems as if it will never end. For one in Brother Miguel's precarious health, accustomed besides to the almost continual sunshine of his native Ecuador, this had a most depressing effect. "The heavens here always seem to be in tears," he would say with a smile. Later he wrote: "For six months now I have not been able to go out-of-doors and during that brief period I have had attacks of the fever eight times."

With the coming of spring his health began to revive, helped no doubt by the signs of new life to be seen everywhere in nature. This was a new experience for Brother Miguel since in Quito there is continual springlike weather and very little to mark the change of seasons. Writing to Ecuador on June 8, 1908, he described it this way:

*How great are the works of God! How beautiful is the vast countryside here during the winter when the fields, the trees and the rooftops are all covered with a blanket of pure white snow!*

*But now I am completely fascinated by the resurrection of nature. The fresh green of the fields, the majestic bloom of the trees, the sweet and varied melodies of the birds — all of it amazes and delights me. You have to see and hear all this for yourself to get some idea of how splendid the spring can really be. May God be ever blessed!*

But Belgium, for all its charms in springtime, was not Ecuador, and translating textbooks was not as satisfying as preparing young students for their first Holy Communion. He writes:

*Please be good enough to let me know how the first Holy Communion class is coming along. Any news that I can get about this, no matter how little or how much, pleases me more than anything. Let me know, please, when it will take place. I am anxious to know all the details. As you are aware, the love for one's native land is such a noble thing that it will never disappear, not even in heaven.*

Shortly thereafter, Brother Miguel sent to the Brother Director of the Sagrada Familia a packet of holy pictures to distribute to the first communicants as a pledge that they held the principal place in his daily prayers.

Whatever longing and homesickness may be evident in these letters, Brother Miguel managed to conceal it from those around him. Always appearing happy and content, he fended off any suggestion that he might be happier elsewhere with these words: "Whatever God wants, I want." God must have heard him, or someone did, because during the course of the summer the superiors decided that it would be just too much to ask him to endure another Belgian winter. Having come to appreciate both his unusual talent and his delicate health, they came to the conclusion that both would thrive better in a more favorable climate. Accordingly they decided to send him to Spain, assigning him to the newly opened junior novitiate in Premiá de Mar, a small town on the shores of the Mediterranean not far from Barcelona.

Brother Miguel made the journey in the company of a group of junior novices, all of them French, who were in training to live out their Lasallian vocation in missionary lands, especially Latin America. As was the case 20 years before, it might have been possible for Brother Miguel to fulfill a lifelong ambition and stop off at Lourdes en route to Spain. This time it was poor health and difficulty in breathing that made the long detour over the mountains impractical. Disappointed a second time at the chance to visit this famous shrine of his Holy Mother, Miguel replied resignedly, "Never mind, I shall see her in heaven."

Once settled in his new quarters at Premiá de Mar, Brother Miguel seemed very pleased. He wrote to Quito: "Here I am in this little corner of the mother country in a very comfortable house. . . . The Mediterranean is only a few yards away. I can see it from my window and I can hear the roaring of the waves which are sometimes tumultuous. Since the sea is so close, there is always a fresh breeze which moderates the heat during the summer months and makes it quite bearable."

Altogether in the new junior novitiate at Premiá there were 63 junior novices preparing to go on the missions, 18 Spaniards and the rest French. Brother Miguel was assigned to teach Spanish to the 25 juniors in the first class. This occupied a good part of each day; the rest was devoted to writing. He was busier than ever. During this time he was working on a Spanish translation of the Catechism of Pope Pius X, a church history for the elementary schools, and a text in Spanish literature. Many more texts were scheduled than he could ever hope to complete, as he said himself: "They want me to produce as many as a dozen of these textbooks. I doubt that there will be time enough for that." When someone suggested that the books might sell better if they were not so saturated with sentiments of Christian piety, he replied: "If a religious congregation doesn't publish books with a Christian viewpoint, nobody will. If these secular minded people don't like them, then they don't have to buy them."

Granted that the natural climate of Spain was pleasant and healthful, the intellectual and spiritual climate inspirational, the political climate definitely was not. The revolutionary anti-clerical movements that had created such havoc in the Brothers' schools in Ecuador and France caught up once more with Brother Miguel and his confreres in Spain. For those who have grown up in the Anglo-American tradition of political democracy and separation of church and state, it is difficult to understand the passion and the violence of the 19th century anti-clerical movements in countries that were traditionally Catholic. There was just cause on both sides, and both sides went to extremes.

The church was certainly justified in asserting its right to proclaim the gospel and to dispense the means of salvation without interference. But church officials often identified with the ideology of ancient and discredited political structures, consistently resisted social reform, and were too concerned to maintain the religious monopoly of the Roman Catholic Church and privileged status for themselves and those who supported church policy. In reaction, the liberal forces were urging more democratic political structures, greater social equality, religious pluralism and freedom of conscience, as well as some legitimate autonomy for secular institutions. Revolutionary fervor, however, often took the form of uncontrolled violence while anti-clericalism turned completely anti-religious. In the process all sense of nuance was lost, and religious institutes such as the Brothers, no matter how remote from political controversy, no matter how effective in meeting genuine human and religious needs, were identified with the church-state establishment and so became the innocent victims who had to suffer the most.

Brother Miguel had been in Premiá de Mar for just about a year when there was a revolutionary outbreak in nearby Barcelona. On July 26, 1909, the anti-government forces declared a general strike, ostensibly to protest the sending of Spanish troops to subdue the Rif tribes in Africa, but actually to initiate the overthrow of the entire political and religious systems. During the following week, *la semana trágica* as it came to be called, rebel mobs roamed unrestrained through the streets, robbing, looting and burning. Priests and nuns were attacked and cemeteries defiled. Sixteen churches and 44 religious establishments were set on fire. The violence quickly spread to the other towns of Catalonia. In Premiá the rebels closed the factories, disrupted the rail service and brought all public activity to a halt. The streets and the port lay deserted. Danger was everywhere, with convents and monasteries particularly vulnerable in view of the treasures they were popularly presumed to contain.

Caught in this violent situation, the Brothers in the junior novitiate at Premiá were advised to remain where they were, lest the buildings and chapel be left as prey to the looters. The authorities assured them that they would be given all possible protection. Armed sentinels were posted to guard the house. A few rifles were supplied to the older Brothers, some of whom had seen military service and were prepared to have recourse to arms to protect themselves and their young charges. Fortunately that did not prove to be necessary.

On Wednesday, July 28, the danger to the Brothers was brought close to home when the freight station across the street was put to the torch. The fire burned all through the night leaving the Brothers and the junior novices wondering whether they might be next. All they could do was to place themselves under the protection of Our Lady, setting up in a corner of the chapel a statue of Our Lady of the Harbor and taking turns at praying before it around the clock. That evening friends and neighbors had more practical suggestions. Some of them offered to take as many of the junior novices as they could into their homes, but the Director was reluctant to break up the community. Others offered to dress the Brothers in peasant costumes and help them to flee. But where? Rail connections to France had been cut, Barcelona was in flames, and the nearby mountains were filled with brigands. It was finally decided after the evening meal that each of the junior novices would be provided with a knapsack and a supply of food. Then they were all sent to the classrooms to sleep at their desks as best they could. At the first sign of an alarm, they were to leave for the mountains and there to spend the night.

During all this confusion Brother Miguel was the picture of calm, going around among them and reassuring them all: "Don't be afraid. Nothing will happen to us. The Blessed Virgin will be our protection." Some of the more realistic of the novices came to him and said: "Brother, you would find it very difficult to climb up to the mountains. If anything should happen, what will you do?" "I'll remain here," he replied, "I won't be alone as long as Our Lord and the Blessed Virgin are here with me. Just give me the keys to the chapel so that I can protect the Blessed Sacrament. However, I guarantee that no harm will come to us. Our heavenly protectress is more powerful than all the armies of the junta put together." He proved to be right, for the time being at least. The night passed without further incident. After Mass and Communion the next day they all went to bed to get some rest.

It was during the course of that day, July 29, that the revolutionary junta established a control center in Premiá. A group of four of them arrived at the Brothers' house clearly intending to take it over. Despite the explanations and pleas of the Brother Director, the members of the commission insisted that the final decision was not in their hands. Their best suggestion was to hire a boat of some kind and leave by sea for a safer place, France perhaps, or anywhere else. They even went so far as to provide the Brother Sub-Director and the Chaplain with a passport to go to Barcelona to see what arrangements they could make. Detained at least ten times in a seven-hour trip by government forces who thought they were rebel spies, the two emissaries were finally granted an audience with the Captain General in Barcelona. By that time the government had established martial law there. The General said that he did not have enough troops to send a detachment to Premiá but, moved by the Brothers, he agreed to provide a boat and an escort vessel to aid in their evacuation.

In the pre-dawn hours of the following morning the tugboat, *Toro*, and the gunboat, *Temerario*, lay to off the beach at

Premiá, flashing their searchlights over the entire shore before dropping anchor. The powerful lights provided a ray of hope to the frightened youngsters as they watched their Sub-Director and the Chaplain come ashore accompanied by the officials in full uniform. The Brother Director and some of the professors were hesitant. Should they abandon the house and leave it to be pillaged? Or should they remain and risk the lives of the Brothers and the vocations of the junior novices? Seeing their hesitation, the Captain said rather impatiently: "Are you coming with me? Yes or no? I'll give you five minutes to decide." He pointed out that everything would be done to protect the building, but there were simply not enough men to guard such an extensive piece of property. His advice was that they should leave, and with this the Chaplain and many other Brothers agreed. After some hesitation, the Director finally gave his consent to depart.

Before leaving the house, Brother Miguel took the statue of Our Lady of the Harbor from its place in the chapel and set it in a window facing the sea. She would be in charge of the house while they were gone. He set the small statue of the Infant Jesus alongside "to keep her company." Then Brother Miguel took from the tabernacle the ciborium filled with the consecrated hosts and placed it in a small case to carry with them in order to save the Blessed Sacrament from any possible profanation. By 4:30 AM all the Brothers were on the beach and rapidly transferred by small boats to the waiting ships. Before giving the signal to depart, the Captain of the *Temerario* summoned the mayor and the judge of the town to appear before him. He told them: "If anyone dares to lay a finger on that house of the Brothers, I'll be back the very next day with my cannons to blow the town to kingdom come."

Under any other circumstances the short passage to Barcelona over a calm sea in the morning sunlight might have been a pleasant excursion. But the refugees were too overcome with terror and fatigue to do anything more than pray or sleep. Brother Miguel read the *Imitation of Christ* and the subject of the morning mental prayer as if they were all back home in the chapel. One of the lads fell sound alseep with his head resting on the case containing the Blessed Sacrament. Brother

Miguel didn't disturb him but merely remarked: "It's just like the Last Supper when the beloved disciple rested his head on the bosom of our Divine Savior."

Once arrived at Barcelona, the Brothers and their young charges took refuge in the dockside warehouses, the only place that seemed to be safe and available. Brother Miguel and the Chaplain were welcomed into the home of Don José Vivas, a prominent Catholic, who hid the ciborium containing the Blessed Sacrament behind a bible in his library until it could be safely brought to a nearby church on the following day. Meanwhile, as rumors began to circulate that a group of religious were hiding in the dock area, the owners began to fear that their buildings would be attacked. This time a friend of the Brothers came to the rescue and persuaded the owner of a nearby hotel to provide food and shelter to the refugees while preparations were being made to evacuate them to the Balearic Islands.

Unexpectedly another and more satisfactory solution was found. Brother Adolfo Alfredo, the procurator at Premiá, suddenly arrived on the scene, fresh from the Colegio Bonanova on the other side of town where Brother Gabriel-Marie, then Superior General, was presiding at a retreat for the Brothers. The college was located in a remote suburb, relatively safe from the possibility of attack. In any case, the worst of the violence seemed to be ended with the imposition of martial law. Accompanied by a military escort, the Brothers and the junior novices set out on foot across the three miles that separated the port area from the college. Making their way by torchlight in the pre-dawn hours, they saw signs of violence and destruction everywhere with many fires still smoldering. The long trek was particularly difficult for Brother Miguel with his crippled legs but he managed to make it, as he said later, "walking at a child's pace that was not more fatiguing than what I had to do in Quito to prepare the boys for their first Holy Communion." The refugees were greeted enthusiastically at Bonanova by the Superior General and the assembled Brothers, delighted especially at the unexpected pleasure of having the learned, saintly and by now rather famous Brother Miguel in their midst.

After about a week at the Bonanova conditions in Barcelona

returned to near normal, the rail lines were reopened, and it was safe for the group from the junior novitiate to return to Premiá. As they approached the house, Brother Miguel pointed to the window where he had left the statue of Our Lady of the Harbor. "Look there," he said, "you can see that our Blessed Mother is beckoning to us." Then, very excitedly, he cried, "And she is alone! She is all alone!" They asked what he meant. "Well," he replied, "before I left the house I placed two statues in the window, the Infant Jesus and the Blessed Virgin. The Infant Jesus has fallen down. That means that Mary alone assumed the responsibility for the protection of the house." Whatever the reason, the Brothers found that nothing in the house had been disturbed in the least. Very soon the routine schedule of the house was reestablished.

# IX. The End of the Beginning

It was no doubt a great relief to the Brothers to find on their return that their house in Premiá had not been damaged during all the troubles of *la semana trágica*. Whether more subtle damage may have been suffered in the impressionable minds of the young juniors by their exposure to terror and uncertainty is another question. What does seem evident is the strain that the whole experience put on the meager physical resources of Brother Miguel. For all of his exterior and interior serenity, it was inevitable that his frail body should react to the strain of sleepless nights and long journeys on his crippled legs.

None of this was apparent at first, and Brother Miguel settled back easily enough into the routine of writing and teaching. In October of 1909 his work took him for a few days to the novitiate at Bugedo. While there he finally had an opportunity to visit one of the famous shrines of his Mother and Protectress, Our Lady of the Pillar, in nearby Saragossa. Much to his surprise he found that someone had placed the flag of Ecuador in the sanctuary. This gave him an incentive to pray with special fervor for his friends in his native land whom he would never see again. Before leaving the community at Bugedo he expressed his thanks to the Brothers and to his heavenly Mother by composing a hymn dedicated to *Nuestra Señora del Pilar*.

In the following month he made his annual retreat which turned out to be his last. He wrote down his retreat resolutions in his diary under the date of November 27, 1909:

> *Resolutions confided to the Sacred Heart of Jesus through my dearest Mother Mary. . . . I will perform all my duties, both writing and teaching, in union with Jesus, Mary and Joseph, only for the glory of God and to make his holy name more widely known, to make reparation for*

*the injuries I have inflicted on Jesus who loves me so much and for those of sinners everywhere. . . . I will say the* Sub tuum *and the* Ave Maria *before beginning any action and also at the half hour. . . . I will frequently express my trust and love for God, my tender and compassionate Father.*

Toward the end of January, 1910, Brother Miguel caught a bad cold. The Brothers were very concerned and insisted that he remain in bed. "Why are you making such a fuss over me?" he asked. "This is nothing serious." On January 31 he requested that they no longer bring his meals to him: "I'm very grateful to all of you but I don't want you to be bothering about me any further. I feel much better, I'm all right now."

On the morning of Wednesday, February 2, during the morning chapel exercises he had a sudden attack of fever. He tried without success to shake it off. Finally, seized with a violent trembling, he said to the Director: "I don't think I'll be able to stay for Mass. I feel cold all over." The Brothers had to help him back to his bed, and the doctor was called. The diagnosis was bronchitis which the doctor said did not appear to be too serious so long as it did not develop into pneumonia. The very next day there was an inflammation of the lungs and it was clear that the patient was not responding to the prescribed treatment. Through it all, Brother Miguel remained serene and even happy, accepting medicines, injections and the orders of the infirmarian without complaint. Though weakened by fever he said the Rosary aloud and followed as best he could the other community prayers from his bed. When asked how he felt, he would say: "I don't feel too bad, I'm a little bit better today."

Over the course of the following week he lingered on and even at times seemed to improve a bit. But by Monday, February 7, it became clear to the doctor that it was time to have him receive the last sacraments. This he did with great fervor and peace, asking that the junior novices pray that the sacraments might have their full effect in him since this was a great grace the Lord was granting to him. The superiors in the motherhouse had been alerted to his condition and they sent promises of prayers. When informed of their concern, Brother Miguel said: "Please tell Brother Assistant that I gladly offer my life for the well-being of the Institute, for its expansion in Ecuador, and for an end to the opposition to Christian education." When asked whether he was sad to be dying so far from home and his native land, he replied: "No, I am happy to die in Spain since that is the will of God."

By Wednesday his lungs became so congested it was evident that the end was near. The Brothers gathered around his bedside in the early afternoon to recite the prayers for the dying which he seemed to follow. As it became increasingly difficult for him to speak, he was heard to murmur, "I am weak . . . . I am weak." Shortly before two o'clock he was able to say "Jesus, Mary and Joseph, I give you my heart and my soul." These were his last words and a fitting summary of his whole life. Then his body became rigid and his breathing agonized. As the final absolution was imparted by the Chaplain, a great calm came over his face, and he died with a peaceful smile on his lips as if once again he had a vision of his "beautiful lady in a white dress with a mantle of blue."

Two days later he was buried in the Brothers' plot in the cemetery in Premiá de Mar. The inscription read:

*Hermano Miguel de Ecuador*
*Escuelas Cristianas*
*Muerto en la paz del Señor*
*el 9 de febrero de 1910*

# X. Now and Forever

It is not without reason that the death of Brother Miguel can be called the end of a beginning. The entirety of his intense and productive life was only a preliminary phase of that blessed life he now enjoys in eternity and the enduring fame he enjoys in time. If there is one recurrent phrase that was used to describe him by those who came in contact with him, even for a short time, it is the expression, "Brother Miguel is a saint." Now the church is making it official. In this final chapter it is appropriate to trace the stages in the process by which that commonly shared impression has been transformed into a solemn proclamation.

When the news of the death of Brother Miguel reached Ecuador, the whole country shared in the sense of loss. The elaborate obsequies were attended by people in enormous numbers and from every walk of life. Two of his former students, Bishop Pólit and Archbishop Pérez Quiñones, presided over pontifical liturgies in their dioceses. The famous orator priest, Luis Escalante, delivered the funeral oration in Quito and he spared none of the grandiose rhetorical devices in fashion at the time to extol the virtues and accomplishments of this uncomplicated man. As other religious congregations joined with the Brothers in mourning their loss, the external expressions of sorrow were tempered with the deeply felt conviction that Ecuador had a new and powerful intercessor before the throne of heaven. To carry this idea further, a group was quickly formed in Quito known as the *Comité Hermano Miguel*. Composed of distinguished citizens, priests and members of various religious congregations, its avowed purpose was to honor and perpetuate the memory of this holy Brother and so to press for his eventual canonization.

Meanwhile, back at the center of the Institute in Lembecq,

the Brothers were not idle. Only two days after Brother Miguel's death, Brother Paul Joseph proposed that a biography be written, a project that he himself was able to complete within three years.

As time went on, it became increasingly apparent to the superiors that the reputation of Brother Miguel for holiness was spreading rapidly and taking a deep hold on the popular imagination, especially in Spanish-speaking countries. Prompted by the bishops in Ecuador and Spain, some of the cardinals in the Roman Curia let it be known that the time might be ripe for the formal introduction of the cause. Accordingly, in 1922 Brother Imier, Superior General, announced officially that the informative process, required by canon law as a means of gathering all the relevant data, was ready to begin. The Superior appointed as Vice-Postulator for the cause the very same Brother Adolfo Alfredo who had rescued Miguel and the Premiá junior novices from the Barcelona docks.

All the Brothers were invited to send testimonial letters to support the case in any way they could. In the following year the informative process was officially opened in the dioceses of Quito, Cuenca and Barcelona. Before it was over, more than 10,000 pages of documents weighing about 70 pounds had been collected. The Vicar General of Barcelona, appointed as the Promoter of the Faith (popularly known as the "devil's advocate"), revealed later that he suspected all along that the Brothers had let their imaginations run away with them and so he did all he could to damage the case. But he finally admitted that the more he looked at the evidence, the more he became convinced personally that Brother Miguel deserved canonization. It was not until 1935, however, that the preliminary process was considered complete, and Pope Pius XI signed the decree formally introducing the cause into the Court of Rome.

While this was going on, the local committees of civilians in Ecuador were planning memorials of their own. The citizens of Cuenca, where Miguel was born, organized a *Comité Hermano Miguel* modeled on the one in Quito. As their first project they erected a memorial of marble in front of the house where Miguel was born which had since become part of the episcopal residence. They also commissioned a life-size portrait to hang in the house itself. Both were dedicated with great ceremony on July 15, 1923. In 1926 in Quito, the city solemnly installed a memorial plaque of marble in the wall of the school at El Cebollar, with the Archbishop presiding and extolling the virtues of his former teacher.

Things were happening in Spain as well. When the mortal remains of Brother Miguel were laid to rest in the cemetery at Premiá de Mar in 1910, they were not destined to remain at rest for very long. Once the preliminary canonical process was opened, permission was given to transfer the body of Brother Miguel to the Brothers' chapel at Premiá. On May 12, 1925, a huge crowd turned out for the occasion. Civil and church officials and large numbers of people from Barcelona joined the Brothers in the procession from the cemetery back to the chapel. The exhumation showed that the body was fairly well preserved but mummified. Once formally identified, the remains were placed in special caskets and sealed in the chapel wall.

In 1936, with Spain in the midst of bitter civil war, the house at Premiá was pillaged by the rebel forces and had to be abandoned. One day in September of that year, a young man named Salvador Camacho, who had been a Brother for a time and had a great regard for Brother Miguel, alerted the Ecuadorian Consul in Barcelona that the tomb of Brother Miguel had been violated and that the body was in danger of being lost forever. He intimated that he would personally look after the body himself until some permanent arrangement could be made to preserve it.

The Consul, Señor Colón Serrano, acted at once. He telegraphed his government in Ecuador asking for authorization to claim the body. By the time an affirmative reply was received, the Consul was not able to make contact with Camacho and he began to fear that the young man might have made off with the remains. Someone suggested that the body might still be at Premiá and there indeed it was found, still recognizable but badly disarranged. Pictures were taken to guarantee the identity of the remains which were then sealed in a specially prepared urn. After agonizing delays and much diplomatic interplay, permission was finally given for the release, and so the remains of Brother Miguel were free to go home at last.

The return to Ecuador on February 5, 1937, was a triumph. A delegation from the capital and the principal cities assembled at Guayaquil to receive the precious remains. Thousands of people joined in the procession as the urn was carried to the cathedral where a Eucharistic Liturgy was celebrated. Then the entourage made its way up the mountains toward Quito, stopping at the key cities along the way. At Riobamba, a lame man approached the cortege to touch the urn. Immediately he threw away his crutches and was able to walk again.

In Quito, the Archbishop, Carlos María de la Torre, a former student of Brother Miguel and later to become Cardinal, received the relics with great solemnity. Once again there was a great outpouring of the people, an endless flow of oratory, and public rejoicing at the return of a national hero. More cures of varying degrees of verifiability were known to have occurred in favor of those who came forward to venerate the relics. Finally on February 13, 1937, the urn with its precious contents was brought to the Brothers' house in the Magdalena and eventually enclosed in a suitable sarcophagus made of marble from Cuenca, Miguel's native city. It seems that his relics may have come to their final resting place at long last.

In the very next year, on March 11, 1938, the apostolic process was opened in Rome to examine the miracles attributed to the intercession of Brother Miguel. Among the many that were brought forth, the most convincing turned out to be the sudden and dramatic cure of Sister Clementina Flores Cordero, a Dominican nun from the town of Azogues in Ecuador where the Brothers had a school. She had first taken sick in April, 1933, and went for treatment to Quito where she was operated on to have one of her kidneys removed. She seemed to recover sufficiently to return to Azogues in March, 1934. But she was stricken once again and wasted away to the point where her life was despaired of. She later described her condition in her own words:

*Although I seemed to have improved, in July of that year [1934] a burning inflammation of the liver caused me to waste away in a very short time. Continual vomiting and unspeakable pain transformed me into a veritable corpse.*

*I remained in this condition until February of the following year. On February 4, no one would have given two cents for my chance to survive. On that day three doctors examined me and they all agreed saying: "The case is fatal; she can't last much longer." Then they ordered that I be given tranquilizers and drugs so that I might die in peace. "Jesus, Mary," I bristled in my lucid moments, "a nun ought not die under the influence of drugs." On that day they all thought I was already dead and started to pray for my soul. But I was still breathing though death was evidently near.*

At this point the Director of the Brothers' school proposed that a novena be started to Brother Miguel. But the Chaplain replied: "What for? We have made many novenas to all the saints and none of them has heard us." The Director insisted: "Let us make one to Brother Miguel. It was only after 36 novenas that the Little Flower worked the miracle that was accepted for her canonization. Besides, next Saturday will be the 25th anniversary of the death of this Servant of God." The priest agreed and the Brother Director sent a picture of Brother Miguel to Sister Clementina. She described what happened in her own words:

*The Brothers began the novena to Brother Miguel on February 6 and in the hospital they began a series of triduums. On Monday, February 11, I felt a tremendous something inside me, a providential command, an irresistible surge in the depths of my being. I opened my eyes wide and impulsively joined my hands in an attitude of praise and thanksgiving. I was cured. The pain had left me and it was as if a new nature had been poured into my flesh and my bones. And so I returned to life. . . . It was a miracle from the holy Brother. . . . I want to make clear that the only thing I was praying for was that the pain might be diminished and that I might be given the strength to support it without morphine. But Brother Miguel obtained for me more than I asked for. He cured me.*

The transformation astonished everyone. The cure was so instantaneous that the Sister was able to take solid food almost at once. Within a day or two, she was able to get up, after six months in bed, and walk about. Most remarkable of all, she never afterwards showed any signs of withdrawal symptoms or dependency on the morphine that had been given to her in increasingly heavy doses to ease the pain of what was expected to be her final agony. It was this simple but startling event that was to occupy the attention and be subject to the scrutiny of the Roman authorities for the next 20 years.

While the long and complicated canonical process in Rome was moving forward at a steady but cautious pace, the government and the citizenry of Ecuador were busy with plans to commemorate the approaching centennial of Brother Miguel's birth in 1854. As early as 1950, the Chamber of Deputies in Quito passed a series of resolutions to that end. The two principal provisions were: that a suitable monument be erected in the capital city to honor this national hero; that all diplomatic means be used to urge the Holy See to step up the process leading to beatification. In 1954 the government issued a series of five postage stamps honoring Brother Miguel: his portrait with the

*The marble and bronze monument to Brother Miguel erected by the government of Ecuador in the public park in Quito, was dedicated on June 4, 1955.*

title *Lirio Azuayo* ("Lily of Azuay," his native province); the school at El Cebollar where he taught from 1896 to 1907; Brother Miguel with two students; the new monument in Quito; the tomb containing his relics.

The monument to Brother Miguel, erected in the public park in Quito, turned out to be an impressive creation in marble and bronze. It is dominated at the center with a statuary group set laterally on each side. The central bronze group features Brother Miguel with three young students, the two side bronzes at either end depict youngsters on the way to school, the marble reliefs show various scenes from the life of Miguel. The monument was solemnly dedicated on June 4, 1955. The unveiling was preceded by a huge parade of some 30,000 school children. The orators vied with one another to find superlatives to describe "the greatest of all Ecuador's teachers," as the former President of the Republic referred to him. The newspapers ran feature articles and editorials on Brother Miguel, and the entire day was celebrated as one of great national importance.

By erecting such an imposing monument, the people of Ecuador had done all in their power to honor the memory of Brother Miguel. The next step was up to Rome. The only thing left to do was to await the formal declaration by church authority that this holy Brother and favorite son deserved to be numbered among the blessed. Popular enthusiasm is one thing, however, and the procedures of the Vatican tribunals, quite another. Rome has been called the Eternal City for many reasons but one of them is the eternity that it takes to get anything done. Besides, during the late 1950's and 1960's the church in Rome had more urgent business to attend to: the death of Pope Piux XII in 1958, the brief but revolutionary pontificate of John XXIII, the unprecedented event that was Vatican Council II, and the election of Paul VI in 1963 to complete the work of transition and to guide the church through the difficult transitional years that lay ahead.

There was even talk during this period that canonizations might become a thing of the past. But events proved otherwise. On March 16, 1970, Paul VI issued the decree proclaiming the heroicity of the virtues of the Servant of God, Brother Miguel. On March 25, 1976, the Medical Commission of the Vatican Congregation for the Causes of Saints verified and approved as miraculous the cure of Sister Clementina Flores Cordero. The bishops of Ecuador were successful in their request that the canonical requirement of a second miracle be waived. In effect, there was no further obstacle to the beatification except to schedule it.

The ceremony was set for Sunday, October 30, 1977, in St. Peter's Square in Rome. Sharing the "honors of the altars" with Brother Miguel on that occasion was the Belgian Christian Brother Mutien-Marie, saintly too but very different from Brother Miguel in many ways. In a homily given at Manhattan College in faraway New York, Brother Timothy McCarthy, FSC, then Associate Provincial, compared the two in these words:

> *They came out of two different cultures, Miguel from Ecuador and Mutien from Belgium. Miguel's father was a professor. Miguel was the first boy to join the Brothers in Ecuador. His father opposed his wish to join the Brothers because he thought the Brothers lacked prestige. Mutien-Marie was the son of a blacksmith. His family encouraged his vocation.*
>
> *Miguel was an accomplished teacher. He loved books. He was a distinguished scholar and an esteemed poet. He was elected to the national academy of letters for his many writings on Spanish grammar and philology. He provided prestige to the Brothers. Mutien-Marie found teaching difficult. His initial efforts were so unproductive that some Brothers considered him unfit to remain in the Brotherhood.*
>
> *Although they were different, both Brothers had much in common. Both were bright students. Both were dependable and stable: Miguel taught at one school for 30 years; Mutien-Marie taught and prefected at a boarding school for 58 years. Both were men of prayer and interiority. Both enjoyed teaching religion. Both loved their vocation and were radically committed to living it. Both manifested heroic fidelity to the exact observance of the Rule. . . . Like De La Salle they taught children the human and Christian disciplines. They respected and loved their students . . . . They*

*were gentle, patient, cheerful. They lived to give glory to God.*

Similar sentiments were expressed, very often with Brothers as homilists, at pontifical liturgical celebrations in other parts of the world, as far away, for example, as Australia, where Brother Christian Moe, FSC, stressed the significance of the two Brothers for the "indirect apostolate," that is, the Christian influence of the teacher outside the formal religion class.

These celebrations worldwide, no matter how solemn and locally significant, were only distant echoes of the main event held out-of-doors in St. Peter's Square in Rome. The day was Sunday, October 30, 1977. Despite some early morning rain, there was a huge crowd in attendance: seating was provided for 23,000 persons; the Vatican radio estimated the final total at 50,000. Dominating the scene was an enormous tapestry depicting the two *beati* that was hung over the central loggia in the facade of St. Peter's Basilica. Pope Paul VI personally read the decree of beatification, gave the homily, and presided over the Eucharist with 20 prelates concelebrating. Present also were 24 cardinals, 60 archbishops and bishops, and 200 vested priests to distribute Holy Communion. In addition to the Sistine Choir, there was a special choir composed of 100 Brothers and 100 religious Sisters of various congregations. Seated prominently were Brother Pablo, Superior General, and his two immediate predecessors in that office, Brother Charles Henry and Brother Nicet Joseph.

Brothers were present in the hundreds from all six continents of the globe. From Ecuador came the Cardinal Archbishop of Quito, Pablo Vega Muñoz, together with Ecuador's two archbishops and 12 bishops, government officials, 72 of the 112 Brothers from the District of Ecuador, and a large delegation of some 2,000 Ecuadorians, including Sister Clementina Flores Cordero, whose cure supplied the miracle required for beatification of Brother Miguel. She was quoted as saying: "I don't know how to describe it: my little Brother Miguel raised to the altars! It is marvelous. And all I asked for was that he would reduce the pain so that I would not need morphine. And he gave me a complete miracle. How happy I am to see him on the altars, and with so many people to admire him, and the Pope congratulating me! And how beautiful the church is with the portraits of the two Brothers on the facade. Now I could really die!" The ceremony took up most of the morning. After it was over, the Pope appeared at the window of his apartments, as he customarily does on Sunday noon to recite the *Angelus,* say a few words to the crowds below, and give his blessing. So taken up was he by the excitement of the occasion that, for the first time ever, he forgot to say the *Angelus.* But he did underscore once again the theme of his homily, the meaning of this event for him and for the church in terms of its importance for the Catholic schools. He said:

> *Let us look with happy eyes at these two champions of human and Christian virtues to bestow on the school our highest esteem. It is an incomparable training ground of formation, for the teachers above all. Let us do honor to those who dedicate their lives to the school.*
>
> *Among the professions worthy of human commitment the school has a front-ranking place, precisely because of the formation it demands and instills in those who accept for themselves its scientific, pedagogical, but above all moral and spiritual perfection which they must acquire for themselves in order to impart it to children, adolescents and young people, and infuse it into the morals of society. The teacher, if conscious of and faithful to his mission, is, through his very profession, a benefactor of humanity as is a father, a doctor or a priest.*

In the days immediately following there was held at the generalate of the Institute a triduum of concelebrated pontifical liturgies designed in turn to accommodate pilgrims from Belgium and France, Ecuador and Spain, and then Italy. Special displays were set up in the rooms of the generalate, and formal receptions were held after each of the liturgies. Finally, at the public audience on Wednesday noon, November 2, the Pope again greeted the pilgrims still in Rome, citing each delegation for special attention, expressing once more his affection for the Institute of the Brothers, his praise for the two *beati,* and imparting his blessing to those who had come such great distances to be part of the event.

It often happens that the solemn ceremonies of beatification are followed by a long period of waiting for some further divine sign and its formal recognition as such by church authority before the final step of canonization can proceed. Some of those declared *beati* seem destined to remain so until time itself merges into eternity. Such was not to be the case with Brother Miguel. On the very day of the beatification itself, a sudden and medically unexplainable cure took place, under the most unusual circumstances, that would leave no doubt that the intercessory power of Brother Miguel remains powerful and efficacious.

The beneficiary was Señora Beatriz Gómez de Nuñez, herself a native of Ecuador. Since 1970 she had been losing control over her bodily movements, her vision distorted, and she was unable to walk without support. The disease was diagnosed as myasthenia gravis. Over the course of seven years she went from one doctor to another, from one treatment to another, seeking in vain for relief until it became clear that her condition was incurable.

Throughout all her sufferings she continued to have confidence in the intercession of Brother Miguel. Once the beatification was announced, she resolved, despite her inability to see clearly or to move about on her own, to go to Rome for the solemn ceremonies in St. Peter's Square. She later described what happened in these words:

> The minute I entered the airplane, I experienced a surge of energy that was completely new. During the flight, as a form of prayer, I kept reciting a poem which my son had composed in honor of Brother Miguel. On the day of the beatification, I was overcome with a feeling of indescribable joy. I could see everything clearly and I could look around at will. I did not yet dare to believe it, but I was well again and completely cured. I returned home like a new person. From that day to this I have never had to use any of the medicines that had been prescribed for me.

In August, 1978, the doctors in the Quito hospital, after noting that the myasthenia had been judged incurable, declared Señora Gómez completely cured with no trace whatever of the disease that had ravaged her for seven years. At the conclusion of the formal canonical processes in Quito and in Rome, the final decree approving the miracle and clearing the way for the canonization was approved in Rome on April 7, 1984, appropriately enough the day assigned for the commemoration in the universal church of St. John Baptist de La Salle.

And so there is a new saint for Ecuador, a country that Brother Miguel loved so dearly and served so well, a country that in its turn had honored his memory, celebrated his achievement, and has never lost confidence in his heavenly intercession. The canonization is an occasion for great rejoicing among all Ecuadorians, but for none more so than Sister Clementina Flores Cordero and Señora Beatriz Gómez and the other beneficiaries of his miracles, as well as for his surviving relatives among whom is none other than Señor León Febres Cordero, recently elected president of Ecuador, whose great-grandfather was the brother of the grandfather of Brother Miguel.

There is a new saint, too, for the universal church and especially for the Institute of the Brothers of the Christian Schools to venerate, to imitate and to petition for divine assistance in the challenges that lie ahead. And so we pray the Lasallian litany: St. John Baptist de La Salle, pray for us. St. Benilde, pray for us. St. Miguel, pray for us. Blessed Solomon, pray for us. Blessed Mutien-Marie, pray for us. Live, Jesus, in our hearts forever!

Printed in Great Britain
by Amazon

61365036R00059